Pray Like a Warrior:
Spiritual Combat & War Room Prayer Guide

ISBN-13: 978-1-950782-23-9 (Holy Water Books)

HOLY WATER BOOKS
At the unexpected horizons of the New Evangelization

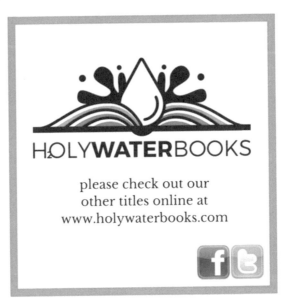

please check out our
other titles online at
www.holywaterbooks.com

Cover design by Holy Water Books

Unless otherwise noted, all Biblical citations and quotes found in this book are taken from the Revised Standard Version (CE) of Sacred Scripture.

PRAY LIKE A PRAYER WARRIOR: Spiritual Combat and War Room Prayer Guide

TABLE OF CONTENTS

INTRODUCTION

I have designed this book to be easily approachable, no matter what Christian tradition you are coming from. Fighting and overcoming the snares of the devil is the common fight of all Christians. In this, we are One Army, One Body of Christ.

Here is the general outline of this book. First, you will put on the **Armor of God**, as St. Paul instructs in the sixth chapter of his Letter to the Ephesians.

Next, you will learn to create your "War Room Prayer Strategy".

Chapter three is collection of prayers. No matter what you are feeling – anger, fear, stress – you will find a prayer tailored to your needs.

In chapter four, you will learn how to wield the **Sword of Truth**, which is Scripture. You will learn how to pray with Scripture to defeat the devil and grow in God's love. A relationship with Jesus Christ is the absolute best way to defeat the Devil. We're not just hanging out with the biggest kid on the block, we are *becoming* Him through the transformative power of God's grace.

Once we learn how to wield the Sword of Truth, I will provide a number of other great Bible verses to meditate on and learn about spiritual warfare. Next, you will find great quotes and teachings from holy men and women. I will also equip you with powerful prayers to banish the Devil and all the evil ones who prowl about the world seeking the ruin of souls. These are extremely powerful and awesome ways to invoke the Name of Christ. These are found in chapters five, six, and seven.

Lastly, I have given you excerpts from *the* classic work on spiritual combat. It has been tested by years and years, even centuries, of use. Many of the most holy men and women have sworn by the tactics found in Lorenzo Scupoli's book.

In the end, I hope this book will strengthen you against temptation. Now more than ever, we need protection from evil. We need holy men and women to lead their families, their communities, their nations, and even their churches back to Christ.

This is a perilous time for us all. Ready your Prayer War Room.

CHAPTER ONE:
How to Arm Yourself
for Spiritual Battle

Be sober, be watchful. Your adversary the devil prowls around like a roaring lion, seeking someone to devour. (1 Peter 5:8)

So how should we approach battle with a "roaring lion"? Should we go into battle in jeans and a t-shirt? Or something more? Ask yourself, how a knight would prepare himself for battle, a knight like St. George who slayed the dragon.

Saint Paul describes how we can arm ourselves for spiritual battle in his Letter to the Ephesians, chapter 6, verses 10-20, below. To "quench all the flaming darts of the evil one," we are to take on the "Whole Armor of God":

Finally, be strong in the Lord and in the strength of his might. Put on **the whole armor of God,** that you may be able to stand against the wiles of the devil. For we are not contending against flesh and blood, but against the principalities, against the powers, against the world rulers of this present darkness, against the spiritual hosts of wickedness in the heavenly places. Therefore, take the whole armor of God, that you may be able to withstand in the evil day, and having done all, to stand. Stand therefore, having girded your loins with truth, and having put on **the breastplate of righteousness,** and having shod your feet with the equipment of the gospel of peace; above all taking **the shield of faith, with which you can quench all the flaming darts of the evil one.** And take **the helmet of salvation**, and **the sword of the Spirit**, which is the word of God. Pray at all times in the Spirit, with all prayer and supplication. To that end keep alert with all perseverance, making supplication for all the saints, and also for me, that utterance may be given me in opening my mouth boldly to proclaim the mystery of the gospel, for which I am an ambassador in chains; that I may declare it boldly, as I ought to speak.

Awake the knight within you! Jesus Christ equips us for battle against evil with the following four items, which we will discuss in detail below:

- The Shield of Faith
- The Breastplate of Righteousness
- The Sword of the Word
- The Helmet of Salvation

The Shield of Faith

In preparing the Christian community in Ephesus for spiritual battle, Saint Paul wrote, "above all taking the shield of faith, with which you can quench all the flaming darts of the evil one" (Eph. 6:16).

Why would Paul describe faith as a shield?

The first instrument for the Christian knight is a shield forged in the virtue of faith. Faith begins with the grace to believe in God, in all that He has said and revealed to us. Faith is the first of the theological virtues. The theological virtues have God as their origin, their motive, and their object. Faith calls for concrete actions. We should profess our faith, confidently bear witness to it, and spread it.[1]

It makes perfect sense then to emphasis faith as the primary ingredient in our first line of defense. Like a shield, faith must be firmly grasped and held before us a barrier between ourselves and the Enemy. When the Shield of Faith is wielded well and without fear, it deflects the doubts and accusations that the Devil hurls at us.[2]

Again, "in *all* circumstances," Saint Paul tell us, "hold faith as a shield, to quench all the flaming arrows of the evil one". This is a ringing call and apostolic summons to spiritual combat. This is especially true when the basic building blocks of a healthy society – marriage and family – are under attack.

The Breastplate of Righteousness

St. Paul is quoting the Book of Wisdom when he encourages us to put on the "Armor of God", 5:17-20:

> The Lord will take his zeal as his whole armor, and will arm all creation to repel his enemies; He will put on righteousness as a breastplate, and wear impartial justice as a helmet; He will take holiness as an invincible shield, and sharpen stern wrath for a sword, and creation will join him to fight against the madmen."

---

[1] Catechism of the Catholic Church, paragraphs 1814, 1816, and 1840.
[2] Thigpen, Paul, *Manual of Spiritual Warfare,* p. 58.

St. Paul is calling us to lead a life of holiness. The most valuable treasure a person can have is a life of righteousness, of purity.

Jesus came to this world to fulfill all righteousness (Mt 3:15). The life of St. Joseph, too, is summed up by saying that he was a righteous man (Mt 1:19). The life of a righteous person stands as a challenge to the sinners. Like St. Joseph, who listen as God speaks to him in his dreams, a righteous person will guide his family and community out of harm's way, even as St. Joseph led the Holy Family away from King Herod's slaughter and into Egypt.

The kingdom of heaven belongs to those who are persecuted for righteousness sake (Mt 5:10). The lives of martyrs underline the fact that the righteous are not afraid even of death.

One who has worn the breastplate of righteousness does not have to fear any adversary. It will always safeguard him.

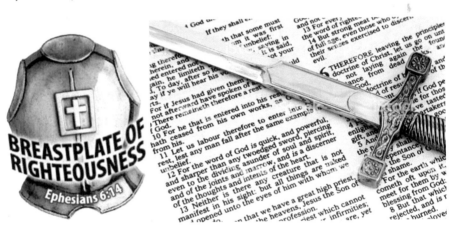

The Sword of the Word

Satan and his minions most likely know the Word of God better than we do, as Satan quoted Scripture effortlessly when he tempted Christ in the wilderness (Matt. 4:1-11). Satan is actually terribly clever in his mis-use and omissions from Scripture. Satan quotes Psalm 91 to tempt Jesus, verses 11 and 12:

For he will give his angels charge of you
    to guard you in all your ways.
On their hands they will bear you up,
    lest you dash your foot against a stone.

Satan skips the next verse, which he would have known very well since the Jewish rabbis used in for exorcisms (the "Exorcism Psalm" provided in Chapter One). Satan skips verse 13 about crushing the serpent, i.e. Satan, under foot:

You will tread on the lion and the adder,
the young lion and the serpent you will trample under foot.

Though Satan could not conceal his identity and intentions from Jesus, St. Paul warns us "even Satan disguises himself as an angel of light" (2 Cor. 11:14).

Therefore, we need to take up "the sword of the Spirit, which is the word of God" (Eph. 6:17).

Memorize God's Word. Read God's Word. Listen to the Word as the Virgin Mary did, who "kept all these things, pondering them in her heart" (Luke 2:19). The sword of Scripture can help you resist temptation and sin.

In the following chapters, we will provide several important Scripture verses to ponder and memorize.

The Helmet of Salvation

We Christians must guard what we allow through the "eye gate" of our minds. As in the Garden of Eden, what we see can lead us into temptation. The fruit of the tree of knowledge of good and evil was described as "a delight to the eyes."

To protect what goes into our minds, we must "take the helmet of salvation" and put it on (Eph. 6:17).

The ultimate human happiness is eternal life found in the kingdom of heaven. The only way for one to meet that objective fully is to place total trust in the promises of Christ, "relying not on our own strength, but on the help of the grace of the Holy Spirit."[3]

In a word, *hope*.

Hope serves not simply as a source for our desires. Hope is a great source of renewal. Hope guards us against discouragement, sustains us during times of abandonment, opens in our hearts the anticipation of eternal beatitude, purifies our activities by aligning them to the order of the heavenly Kingdom, preserves us against selfishness, and leads to the happiness that flows from charity.

Prayer plays a critical role, too. In particular, the Our Father, or Lord's Prayer, which is "the summary of everything that *hope* leads us to desire".

The hope of salvation is "essential for protecting the mind [...] against the temptation to despair."[4]

Immortal hope is an antidote to *mortal* hopelessness. Hopelessness "open(s) our minds wide to all the thoughts the Enemy seeks to plant there." Hopelessness also slackens our will to fight over time.

But *hope* – hope reigns eternal.

Conclusion

St. Paul equips the Christian, but it's not enough to merely know about these pieces of armor. A Christian must to "take up" the full armor of God. Practice these armors until they become habits. It takes time and practice to wield a sword. The unwary might accidentally chop off the servant's ear, as Saint Peter did during Jesus' arrest. When the enemy attacks, you will be ready.

The following chapters will further equip you for battle and guide you in your practice of the Faith and swordsmanship.

In the succeeding chapter, "Most Powerful Prayers for Spiritual Warfare," you will find a great way to pray for each of these armaments, one by one, and Ephesians 6, verse by verse.

---

[3] *Catechism of the Catholic Church*, paragraphs 1817-1818.
[4] Thigpen, 58.

CHAPTER TWO:
How to Create Your
War Room Prayer Strategy

We have put on the Armor of God, as described in Ephesians 6 and the previous chapter. Now, we are ready for the next key battle strategy to defeating the evil one in prayer: developing a War Room Prayer Strategy. You might be asking yourself …

What is a War Room Prayer Strategy?[5]

The War Room. It's where prayer strategy happens. Where the fight against sin and temptation gets real. Where battle lines are drawn.

Just as a military needs a command center, a headquarters, you need a "inner room" or a quarters in your own head. Christians need a sacred space where you go to battle against a very real enemy.

You need a war room prayer strategy.

Have you seen or heard of the movie *War Room* starring Priscilla Shirer? This is where the idea of a "War Room" comes from, but it is not a new idea.

War Room is a reminder of the authority promised to us in 2 Corinthians 10:7-9:

---

[5] Adapted from Jennie McChargue, rockthis.org

Look at what is before your eyes. If anyone is confident that he is Christ's, let him remind himself that as he is Christ's, so are we. For even if I boast a little too much of our authority, which the Lord gave for building you up and not for destroying you, I shall not be put to shame.

Jesus gives us power over evil! We must never forget this. Merely by invoking the Name of Jesus, we are given power and authority over evil.

Remember, also, the power we possess according to 2 Timothy 1:7:

For God did not give us a spirit of timidity but a spirit of power and love and self-control.

It's time to claim the power and authority given to us by His Supreme Majesty as His adopted sons and daughters.

How to Create a War Room Prayer Strategy:

BE PREPARED

This book is full of wisdom and quotes from the Bible and holy people, but for this section we're doing something a little different. Here is some battle-hardened wisdom from Ulysses S. Grant to help us develop our War Room Strategy:

The art of war is simple enough. Find out where your enemy is. Get at him as soon as you can. Strike him as hard as you can, and keep moving on.

A very simple, pragmatic man, Grant gives us a simple formula: (1) Find your enemy, (2) Strike quickly, (3) Strike hard, and (4) Keep moving.

Find your enemy: You know where the enemy is. He is prowling about like a lion. He is where your joy is, looking to steal it. He wants to devour your life and destroy your family through you.

Strike quickly: Don't wait. Act now. We can move much faster than armies. It takes only a moment to call on the Name of Jesus, to pray the "Our

Father", or to trace the Sign of the Cross on your forehead. These are each fine choices for an opening salvo. Any one of these can deal a mortal blow to your enemy.

Strike hard: Jesus has empowered you to call on His angels for help. God has given each of us, specifically, a guardian angel to call on. You've been given permission to wield "the weapons of righteousness for the right hand and for the left" (2 Corinthians 6:7). It's okay to battle. We are *called* to battle. In fact, God calls us to it in Ephesians 6, as discussed in the previous chapter. The "Armor of God" is not meant to be decorative.

As a new creation in Christ, confidently believe that your prayers are powerful. Be **bold** and stand unveiled, for you stand under the banner of Christ, 2 Corinthians 3:12-13:

> *Since we have such a hope, we are very bold, not like Moses, who put a veil over his face so that the Israelites might not see the end of the fading splendor.*

Moses' face shone with the light of God, and yet he veiled it. Unveil your face when facing the enemy. Let the light of your face shine in the darkness.

Keep moving: Time spent in the war room will sharpen and enlighten your spiritual senses, making you keenly aware of the enemy's approach. Catch his lies before you fall prey to them.

BE WELL-POSITIONED

The enemy will attack. There's no secret to the evil one's strategy. It is not a matter of if, but when he will attack. His timing is awful and his pursuit relentless. He will take advantage of every weakness, weak moment, person, and situation in your life. He will hit where it hurts. His objective to destroy you by whatever means necessary.

Here is more battle-hardened wisdom from the author of *The Art of War,* the great military strategist Sun Tzu:

> *The art of war teaches us to rely not on the likelihood of the enemy's not coming, but on our own readiness to receive him; not on the chance of his not attacking, but rather on the fact that we have made our position unassailable.*

Are you ready? Is your "position unassailable"? What position can you take that will prevent the devil from ever reaching you?

Consider James 4:7-8:

> *Submit yourselves therefore to God.*
> *Resist the devil and he will flee from you.*
> *Draw near to God and he will draw near to you.*

Put yourself under the banner of God, and the devil will flee from you. Draw near to God, and you will find his fortress and legions of angels encircling you. God, Himself, will come close to you.

But this takes practice. Turning towards God is a difficult pivot to make when encircled by temptation and despair. Time spent in the war room prepares you for the coming battle. It builds endurance, strengthens your spiritual stamina, and prepares you for the coming storms.

Remember, Jesus has already defeated death and sin. He has conquered the grave. The enemy has already been defeated.

Develop and practice your strategy for calling on His aid when under siege. Like the character Boromir in Tolkien's classic *Fellowship of the Ring*, blow the horn of Gondor, the horn of Christ, and your allies will come to your aid.

Figure 1: Boromir blowing the Horn of Gondor when surrounded by enemies at Amon Hen

STAY IN COMMUNITY

Speaking of "fellowship," God has prepared us for a community of believers and fellowship within the Body of Christ. God calls us to community. The devil wants us to be alone. He hopes to divide and conquer, and so destroy us. We are not meant to live life alone. Christ surrounded himself with the love and support of faithful friends. And Saint Paul tell us to call on this great "cloud of witnesses" that surrounds us for help.

Jesus feasted with his disciples. In times of struggle, Jesus prayed with them, too. Jesus went to His own War Room, the Garden of Gethsemane, on the night before His crucifixion. He did not go alone, either. He brought with Him Peter, James, and John, the inner circle of His Apostles.

Jesus was ministered to by angels and his most trusted friends in the Original War Room:

Figure 2: The Angel ministering to Jesus in the Garden of Gethsemane

This same dynamic can be found in soldiers rallying during times of war and generals preparing for battle with their key lieutenants. This time spent in fellowship helps the army work as **One** and prevents the devil from dividing them.

None of us can do it alone. Community helps us live and pray as witnesses to the resurrected Christ. "The community of believers was of one heart and mind (*cor unum et anima una*)" (Acts 4:32).

Nineteenth-century military strategist Carl von Clausewitz understood the role of troops and unity in winning the war:

> *Tactics is the art of using troops in battle; strategy is the art of using battles to win the war.*

The time you spend in fellowship with Christ, with your prayer partners, with your heavenly intercessors rallying in the war room will increase your chances of victory in battle. Invite friends to establish war room space in their homes so that they may join you in the war against the enemy.

BE IN YOUR WAR ROOM

A War Room is defined as a location where teams of communications experts monitor and listen to dispatches and transmissions describing allied and enemy troop movements. It is the place where leaders respond to communications and form prudent opinions to determine the best course of action.

What is the most essential and precious communication to be heard and received in the War Room? The word of God, whether it is spoken in our hearts or found in Scripture.

The War Room is the precious, sacred space for the Christian to come before the Lord. This is the place where we remove our sandals, like Moses, and stand before the burning bush, the Presence of God. Here, we communicate with God, hear God's voice, and respond to God's promptings in our hearts.

Develop a habit of bringing your struggles to the War Room, that is, to God. There is no struggle too great or too small for the War Room. Meet God here on your knees, develop your strategies with Him, and learn to submit to and trust His will.

What kind of struggles can you take to the War Room? Are you struggling with your spouse? Take your marriage to the War Room. Has your child fallen away from Christ? Take your parenthood into the War Room. Are you or a loved one sick? Bring them to the War Room for healing.

The more time spent in the War Room, the more the War Room will become part of you. The ultimate goal, as Saint Paul describes, is to "pray without ceasing". With God's grace, you will be within your War Room "without creasing".

CHAPTER THREE:
Prayers for the War Room

Ometimes the hardest part of the War Room is getting inside it. Even if it's a physical space, it can be difficult to be fully inside the War Room when your thoughts and worries are elsewhere.

Here are some prayers that might help you bring yourself fully into War Room. These prayers are for you and your loved ones. They are also for those that are hard to love, but are all the more in need your prayers – for their sake and your own.

What emotions are you feeling that preventing you from fully entering your War Room? What are your needs? Here are a host of feelings you may be experiencing that are either distracting you from prayer from can help you enter into it:

CALMING A TROUBLED HEART

Loving God,
Please grant me peace of mind
And calm my troubled heart.
My soul is like a turbulent sea.
I can't seem to find my balance,
So I stumble and worry constantly.
Give me the strength and clarity of mind
To find my purpose and walk the path
You've laid out for me.
I trust Your Love, God,

And know that You will heal this stress.
Just as the sun rises each day
Against the dark of night.
Please bring me clarity with the light of God.
In Your Name I pray.
Amen.

ANGER[6]

Lord, You are slow to anger and abounding in love. In the places in my heart where anger resides, grace me to become aware of them, to repent of the ways I have clung to anger, and grow Your love and patience there instead.

PANIC – "A PRAYER FOR SOOTHING PANIC ATTACKS"

Dear God,
I come before You to lay my panic and anxiety at Your feet.
When I'm crushed by my fears and worries, remind me of Your power and Your grace.
Fill me with Your peace as I trust in You and You alone.
I know I can't beat this on my own, but I also know that I have You, Lord, and You have already paid the ultimate price to carry my burdens.
For this I thank you.
Amen.

PRIDE – "LITANY OF HUMILITY"

O Jesus, meek and humble of heart, *Hear me.*
From the desire of being esteemed, *Deliver me, O Jesus.*
From the desire of being loved, *Deliver me, O Jesus.*
From the desire of being extolled, *Deliver me, O Jesus.*
From the desire of being honored, *Deliver me, O Jesus.*
From the desire of being praised, *Deliver me, O Jesus.*
From the desire of being preferred to others, *Deliver me, O Jesus.*
From the desire of being consulted, *Deliver me, O Jesus.*
From the desire of being approved, *Deliver me, O Jesus.*
From the fear of being humiliated, *Deliver me, O Jesus.*
From the fear of being despised, *Deliver me, O Jesus.*

[6] April Motl, "Overcoming Strongholds," crosswalk.com

17

From the fear of suffering rebukes, *Deliver me, O Jesus.*
From the fear of being calumniated, *Deliver me, O Jesus.*
From the fear of being forgotten, *Deliver me, O Jesus.*
From the fear of being ridiculed, *Deliver me, O Jesus.*
From the fear of being wronged, *Deliver me, O Jesus.*
From the fear of being suspected, *Deliver me, O Jesus.*
That others may be loved more than I,
Jesus, grant me the grace to desire it.
That others may be esteemed more than I,
Jesus, grant me the grace to desire it.
That, in the opinion of the world, others may increase and I may decrease,
Jesus, grant me the grace to desire it.
That others may be chosen and I set aside,
Jesus, grant me the grace to desire it.
That others may be praised and I go unnoticed,
Jesus, grant me the grace to desire it.
That others may be preferred to me in everything,
Jesus, grant me the grace to desire it.
That others may become holier than I, provided that I may become as holy
as I should, *Jesus, grant me the grace to desire it.*
Amen.

ANXIETY – "THE SERENITY PRAYER"

God, grant me the serenity
to accept the things I cannot change,
the courage to change the things I can,
and the wisdom to know the difference.
Living one day at a time,
enjoying one moment at a time;
accepting hardship as a pathway to peace;
taking, as Jesus did,
this sinful world as it is,
not as I would have it;
trusting that You will make all things right
if I surrender to Your will;
so that I may be reasonably happy in this life
and supremely happy with You forever in the next. Amen.

Unforgiveness & Bitterness[7]

Lord, help me see the unhealed places in my soul that need forgiveness. Enlighten my perspective so I can see my unforgiveness the same way You do and to desire to give forgiveness with the same passion You do. Help me forgive others just like You have forgiven me!

Weakness – "Prayer for Strength" (from Psalm 27:1b)

Dear Jesus,
You are the strength of my life;
You are my rock, my fortress and my protector;
Therefore, whom shall I be afraid?
You are my shield,
My strong-tower and my stronghold.
I will call to You because
You are worthy to be praised.
So, Father, I thank you for being my strength
And My God in whom I trust.
Amen.

Trust – "The Litany of Trust"

From the belief that I have to earn Your love, *Deliver me, Jesus.*
From the fear that I am unlovable, *Deliver me, Jesus.*
From the false security that I have what it takes, *Deliver me, Jesus.*
From the fear that trusting You will leave me more destitute,
Deliver me, Jesus.
From all suspicion of Your words and promises, *Deliver me, Jesus.*
From the rebellion against childlike dependency on You, *Deliver me, Jesus.*
From refusals and reluctances in accepting Your will, *Deliver me, Jesus.*
From anxiety about the future, *Deliver me, Jesus.*
From resentment or excessive preoccupation with the past, *Deliver me, Jesus.*
From restless self-seeking in the present moment, *Deliver me, Jesus.*
From disbelief in Your love and presence, *Deliver me, Jesus.*
From the fear of being asked to give more than I have, *Deliver me, Jesus.*
From the belief that my life has no meaning or worth, *Deliver me, Jesus.*
From the fear of what love demands, *Deliver me, Jesus.*

---

[7] Ibid.

From discouragement, *Deliver me, Jesus.*

That You are continually holding me, sustaining me, loving me,
Jesus, I trust in You.
That Your love goes deeper than my sins and failings and transforms me,
Jesus, I trust in You.
That not knowing what tomorrow brings is an invitation to lean on You,
Jesus, I trust in You.
That You are with me in my suffering, *Jesus, I trust in You.*
That my suffering, united to Your own, will bear fruit in this life and the next, *Jesus, I trust in You.*
That You will not leave me orphan, that You are present in Your Church,
Jesus, I trust in You.
That Your plan is better than anything else, *Jesus, I trust in You.*
That You always hear me and in Your goodness always respond to me
Jesus, I trust in You.
That You give me the grace to accept forgiveness and to forgive others
Jesus, I trust in You.
That You give me all the strength I need for what is asked
Jesus, I trust in You.
That my life is a gift, *Jesus, I trust in You.*
That You will teach me to trust You, *Jesus, I trust in You.*
That You are my Lord and my God, *Jesus, I trust in You.*
That I am Your beloved one, *Jesus, I trust in You.*

FEAR – "A PRAYER TO CAST OUT FEAR"

I know that worrying gets me nowhere.
Yet I still allow worry and anxiety to consume me.
In times such as these,
Lord Jesus,
I ask you to grant me
A great amount of strength, faith, and courage
To fight off the doubt and fear
Within my mind and heart.
Faith casts out fear
While fear casts out faith.

HOPELESSNESS – "ACT OF HOPE"

My God, relying on your
infinite goodness and promises,
I hope to obtain pardon of my sins,
Help of your grace,
And life everlasting
Through the merits of Jesus Christ,
My Lord and Redeemer
Amen.

STRONGHOLDS[8]

Heavenly Father, I feel the enemy's grip on my neck. His lies are loud. His schemes are real. He seeks to steal my joy, destroy my home, and wreck my life. My strength is failing, and my hope is weak. I need you, Lord. Holy Spirit make your presence known. Fill my heart. Fill every room in my house. Be the light that I desperately need. In Jesus' name I pray. Amen!

STRESS – "A PRAYER FOR UNBURDENING THE MIND"

Dear Loving Lord,
I am feeling stress, I am worried.
Too many things occupy my mind.
Won't you help me?
Show me, Lord,
Your order and Your plans are eternal.
Let me trust in Your Will alone.
Your Word tells me where there is love,
there is no fear.
Let me be filled with Your Love.
The perfect love
That tells me I am not condemned,
but I am saved.
I can do all things through You.
You strengthen me.
In Jesus name,
Amen.

---

[8] Ibid., McChargue.

21

Scott L. Smith, Jr.

INTERCESSION[9]

Lord Jesus, I come to you today and thank you for the privilege of praying for others. I've been the recipient of others' prayers so often, I understand how powerful intercessory prayer can be. I ask you first to cleanse my heart and show me if there is any unconfessed sin in my own life so that my prayers for others will not be hindered. I thank you that through your name, I can come boldly before you and pray with confidence, according to your will and know that you hear me.

I lift up those in my neighborhood, in my city, and in my church. Begin with those who follow you, and help them influence others for good. Let them be salt and light, pointing others to you. Deepen their love for you and for the people around them. Guard them from hypocrisy or from giving in to temptations that could harm the cause of Christ. Raise up leaders who will serve you faithfully at all costs. Turn the hearts of fathers toward their children, and families toward you. Help them to exemplify your values, and make them bold in their faith. Strengthen my own family, and those closest to me, Lord. May our love for you help us to love and forgive others and make a difference in our world.

I pray for teachers, for students, and for all those in authority and leadership, both locally and throughout the world. Give them your mind, and surround them with godly counselors who will exercise integrity and work for justice, morality, and freedom. Help them to esteem you, not dismiss you. Send revival, Lord.

I pray for the lost, the hurting, the lonely, the sick, the bereaved, and those who are imprisoned—behind both visible and invisible walls. Send your comfort, your peace, and your calming presence to those who are without hope. Protect the defenseless, and hold them close to your heart. I pray for laborers to tell the good news of Jesus to people around our world. Jesus, my heart cries out for persecuted believers, too. Make them brave, and give them your powerful protection. I pray you will bring swift justice to those who want to destroy the innocent and those who carry your name. Bind the power of Satan, and strengthen believers everywhere.

---

[9] Rebecca Barlow Jordan, "An Intercessory Prayer - Encouraging Others," Crosswalk.com

22

So many needs, Jesus, but you are adequate for every need. Your name is powerful, and your power is great. So it's in your name that I pray—and believe. Amen.

SALVATION – "TAKE AND RECEIVE PRAYER", ALSO CALLED "THE SUSCIPE"

Take, Lord, and receive all my liberty,
my memory, my understanding,
and my entire will,
All I have and call my own.
You have given all to me.
To you, Lord, I return it.
Everything is yours; do with it what you will.
Give me only your love and your grace,
that is enough for me.

RESCUE & SHELTER – "THE *ANIMA CHRISTI* PRAYER"

Soul of Christ, sanctify me.
Body of Christ, save me.
Blood of Christ, inebriate me.
Water from the side of Christ, wash me.
Passion of Christ, strengthen me.
O Good Jesus, hear me.
Within your wounds, hide me.
Permit me not to be separated from you.
From the wicked foe, defend me.
At the hour of my death, call me
And bid me come to you,
That with your saints I may praise you
Forever and ever.
Amen.

FORGIVENESS – "PRAYER FOR PEACE AND CALM" BY JOHN GREENLEAF WHITTIER

Dear Lord and Father of humankind,
Forgive our foolish ways;
Reclothe us in our rightful mind,

Scott L. Smith, Jr.

In purer lives Thy service find,
In deeper reverence, praise.

Drop Thy still dews of quietness,
Till all our strivings cease;
Take from our souls the strain and stress,
And let our ordered lives confess
The beauty of Thy peace.

Breathe through the heats of our desire
Thy coolness and Thy balm;
Let sense be dumb, let flesh retire;
Speak through the earthquake, wind, and fire,
O still, small voice of calm.

REPENTANCE – "ACT OF CONTRITION"

O my God,
I am heartily sorry for having offended Thee,
and I detest all my sins,
because I dread the loss of heaven, and the pains of hell;
but most of all because they offend Thee, my God,
Who are all good and deserving of all my love.
I firmly resolve, with the help of Thy grace,
to confess my sins, to do penance,
and to amend my life.
Amen.

CHAPTER FOUR:
How to Pray With Scripture for Spiritual Warfare

We have put on the Armor of God, as described in Ephesians 6, and we have developed our War Room Prayer Strategy. Now, we are ready for the next key battle strategy to defeating the evil one in prayer.

This brings us to the first important point: God really wants to speak to us, each one of us. No one is excluded. It does not matter what we have done. Furthermore, God wants to reveal His love for us, each one of us, and no one is excluded. It does not matter what we have done. Even if we have *just* given into temptation, NOW is always the time for prayer and God's love.

God's love is the key to completely overwhelming the snares and traps of the Devil.

Before we even existed, God loved us. He created us out of love, He redeemed us out of love and by His love, He continues to call us back to Himself. Like the Prodigal Son (Luke 15), no matter how far we have wandered, there is a celebration and warm welcome awaiting us in the Father's house, our true home.

That is the "tone of voice" we can expect from God when we pray with Sacred Scripture. We can always ask the question, "How is God revealing His love to me through this passage of Scripture?"

I am going to walk you through an ancient way of praying with Bible verses. It's called *Lectio Divina*.

How to Defeat the Devil
with Scripture: *Lectio Divina*

STEP 1: READING

The first step of *lectio divina* is opening our Bible to a page of Scripture and reading. There are many ways to choose what Scripture we begin with. For the purposes of Spiritual Warfare, the next chapter is full of Bible verses that I have picked out for just this purpose. Another great place to start is the four Gospels of Matthew, Mark, Luke or John, because it is easiest to encounter God through the Gospels. Another great choice is the readings for the day. There is a daily cycle of Gospel and Old Testament readings selected for Catholic Mass or other church services.

We do not need to read a large amount of Scripture. The purpose of *lectio divina* is different than a bible study. With *lectio*, we are not trying to become Scripture scholars, we are simply trying to draw close to God and hear His voice speaking to us personally. So, all you really need is just a paragraph of Scripture to start with. Sometimes just a single verse will do! Remember, the infinite God is to be found in *every* verse of the Bible.

After we have selected a passage of Scripture, we begin to read slowly. Let me emphasize: *slowly*. For prayer, it is very important to slow ourselves down, to quiet our minds and hearts, and to become more gentle in our approach to God. We are just nibbling at Scripture right now. The point is to just *be* with Scripture. *Rest* with Scripture, as though you were resting in Jesus' arms. Because Jesus is Scripture. Jesus is the Incarnate Word of God.

We know that God is almighty, but when He speaks, He does not try to dominate us or overwhelm us. This is because He really respects and reverences our freedom. He wants to be sure that we really, really want to hear what He has to say. By becoming very quiet and very gentle inside ourselves, we show Him that we are really interested in listening to Him.

God is like a father watching over a child slowly falling asleep. As we drift into God's own arms, He is very careful not to disturb us.

Transitioning from our world of noise and busyness is a lot like falling asleep. You can't force yourself to pray any more than you can force yourself to fall asleep. You need to slip into the quiet of prayer gently.

Prayer is not just another television channel you can click to. Prayer is waiting in silence for God until such time that you realize His arms were wrapped around you the whole time.

Through *lectio divina*, we enter this gentle quiet by taking a phrase of Scripture and gently repeating it. As we read through the passage, we look for a phrase of Scripture that seems to stand out or that catches our attention. There's no magic to it. Any phrase will work, because God is waiting behind every word. If there is one verse or phrase that seems to be drawing you in, take that one and begin to repeat it quietly to yourself.

STEP 2: MEDITATION

The meditation begins as we start repeating the phrase of Scripture. It is just a gentle repetition in the beginning, like dipping our toes in the water. Soon we will wade in.

The repetition is important because it helps us slow down and focus. When we first enter into prayer, our interior space can be a mess and whirlwind of thoughts. We are conditioned to act, act, act, and do, do, do throughout our day. We need to flip the switch. Let this storm of thoughts dissipate and settle.

This is making us more sensitive to God's Presence. As our focus shifts from the whirlwind of thoughts, we will realize that we are standing before the great immeasurable vista of God's Presence.

We have conditioned our minds to a certain RPM, revolutions per minute. We resist the calm. The whirlwind wants to kick back up again.

Each time we repeat the verse or verses from Scripture, we are tapping down that whirlwind, tamping out the fire of our thoughts. This is how our interior becomes more settled, more calm, and open to God's Presence.

Our thoughts will keep returning to us as gales of wind, but we just keep repeating the Scripture.

Eventually, our minds will stop spinning. Our hearts will quiet. You might even find the flame of God's Presence flicker and erupt in your heart, but this is not always the way of it.

As we repeat the Scripture verse or verses, something else also begins to happen. We begin entering into the Word. We are reflecting on the meaning of the verse. Is a particular word or phrase standing out? Does a certain part touch you, soothe you, excite you, comfort you? Stay with that. That is a guidepost from God, leading you deeper into the mystery.

Take, for example, the Parable of the Prodigal Son. If you were meditating on this passage, any of the following thoughts might capture your imagination or gnaw at your curiosity.

You may be struck by the phrase in Luke 15:20, "So he got up and went back to his father." We might notice the courage of the son to get up and go back. We might feel his fear of rejection. We may learn from his directness in the face of temptations to turn back. We might remember our own sins. We might encounter an experience of being rejected by our own father. We might feel despair and wonder what the point of returning is.

In the midst of all or any of these meditations, we keep repeating, "So he got up and went back to his father."

We know the Prodigal Son's path from here. He was not rejected. He was received with love and a celebration. We might ask ourselves, "What is keeping me from getting up and returning to God, my Father? Am I afraid? Am I despairing?" We can imagine the loving way our Father receives us with open arms.

And again, we repeat the phrase, "So he got back up and went back to his father."

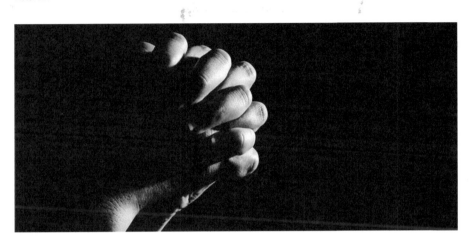

STEP 3: PRAYER

Once you have drank your full of Scripture, you are ready for the next step. The third movement of *lectio divina* is prayer.

In our meditation period, we asked ourselves, "What is God saying to me in this passage?" Now, in prayer, we respond to God.

Still using the example of the Prodigal Son, we might begin to pray with thanking God: "Thank you Father for always receiving me when I get up and return to you."

Or, asking God's forgiveness: "Please forgive me for wandering away from you. Please help me never to wander from you again."

Or, asking God to change us: "Why do I continually fall back into sin? Please help me to be faithful. Please help me always to get up and return to you when I fall."

Or, asking God to help others, intercessory prayer: "Please help all those who fall into sin to get up and return to you."

The important thing in prayer authenticity. What is actually on your mind and heart? Speak from where you really are, not where you think you should be.

God already knows what we need to say. He has known for all time and before Creation, itself. **God is closer to you than you are to yourself!**

So be honest in prayer. Be transparent. God loves to listen to us. He wants to hear what is in our hearts, so we can unburden our hearts. Prayer is not a dissertation or a performance. We are not being graded or judged. This is our time with God. Our feelings, our fears, our hopes, the people we love and care for, whatever is in our hearts – bring *that* to God.

STEP 4: CONTEMPLATION

Through the previous steps, we have hopefully stilled the whirlwind in our hearts and minds. We have entered into silence, as much as we can in the midst of our daily craziness. Nevertheless, we have created some separation between us and the world.

At this point – hopefully, but maybe not always – we can now relax in the loving embrace of God. Just spend some time in His lap or His arms or His hand. The whole world, all the air in your lungs, even your armchair, is God's embrace. Let yourself feel it.

Letting go and resting in God's Presence is the fourth movement of *lectio divina*. This is called contemplation. Contemplation is a loving awareness of God's Presence.

When we feel God close to us, words are no longer needed. God's depths are beyond words. Just rest. Enjoy this other whirlwind of God's loving embrace. Speak to God in and with silence.

This may last for seconds, minutes, or more – hours, if you have them. Days, if you are at that stage of sainthood.

Gradually, we return. We may move back to the original Scripture passage or another one, or back to a previous step, or the close of our prayer time.

POPE FRANCIS ON *LECTIO DIVINA*

Let us conclude by reflecting on Pope Francis's teaching on this form of prayer. The Pope gives us some excellent insights into the distractions and temptations that might arise as we seek to enter into God's Presence:[10]

> There is one particular way of listening to what the Lord wishes to tell us in his word and of letting ourselves be transformed by the Spirit. It is what we call *lectio divina*. It consists of reading God's word in a moment of prayer and allowing it to enlighten and renew us. ...
>
> In the presence of God, during a recollected reading of the text, it is good to ask, for example: 'Lord, what does this text say to me? What is it about my life that you want to change by this text? What troubles me about this text? Why am I not interested in this? Or perhaps: What do I find pleasant in this text? What is it about this word that moves me? What attracts me? Why does it attract me?'
>
> When we make an effort to listen to the Lord, temptations usually arise. One of them is simply to feel troubled or burdened, and to turn away. Another common temptation is to think about what the text means for other people, and so avoid applying it to our own life. It can also happen that we look for excuses to water down the clear meaning of the text. Or we can wonder if God is demanding too much of us, asking for a decision which we are not yet prepared to make.
>
> This leads many people to stop taking pleasure in the encounter with God's word; but this would mean forgetting that no one is more patient than God our Father, that no one is more understanding and willing to wait. He always invites us to take a step forward, but does not demand a full response if we are not yet ready. He simply asks that we sincerely look at our life and present ourselves honestly before him, and that we be willing to continue to grow, aking from him what we ourselves cannot as yet achieve.

---

[10] Pope Francis, *The Joy of the Gospel*, No. 153-154

Scott L. Smith, Jr.

Lectio Divina Example: Ephesians 6 Prayer

Lectio Divina is a very simple prayer method. All you need is a small piece of Scripture and time. You do not need (or want) a step-by-step guide. You want to just plunge into God's depths, "into the deep," as St. Pope John Paul II describes it.

Nevertheless, here is an example of *Lectio Divina* with the specific aim of arming yourself your Spiritual Combat.

The previous chapter included a thorough examination of St. Paul's description of the "Armor of God." Now, here is a way to pray for each of these armaments, one by one, using *lectio divina*-style method, breaking down the verses into bite-sized mediations:[11]

Ephesians 6:10: Finally, be strong in the Lord and in the strength of his might.

Lord, I've never felt weaker or more defeated in the battle against the evil spirits. In your mercy, hold me upright in the strength of your might. Protect me from this evil onslaught and increase my faith that I may not succumb to diabolical temptations. O Incarnate Mercy, embrace your suffering servant with tender strength.

Ephesians 6:11: Put on the whole armor of God, that you may be able to stand against the wiles of the devil.

Lord Jesus, you are the whole armor of the Christian soldier—cover me please. Wherever there is a weak link in my spiritual armor, please heal and restore its integrity. The wiles of the devil are manifold leading me into darkness, discouragement, doubt, and division—even against myself, friends and family. I need your light to see, your encouragement to persevere, and affirmation that, with your grace, I can resist and the enemy will flee.

Ephesians 6:12: For we are not contending against flesh and blood, but against the principalities, against the powers, against the world rulers of this present darkness, against the spiritual hosts of wickedness in the heavenly places.

---

[11] Kathleen Beckham, "Ephesians Six: Prayers in Spiritual Warfare," *Catholic Exchange*.

Eternal Father, what defense do I, a poor sinner, have against powers and principalities, and their wickedness? You have given me your Son Jesus Christ as spiritual armor. Father, graciously place me into the depths of the Sacred Heart, my refuge against this present darkness. If I have succumbed to evil, lead me to repentance, reparation and restoration. I am your unworthy child but the Blood of your Son Jesus is my garment because you willed it. Thank you for your loving, perpetual care.

Ephesians 6:13: Therefore, take the whole armor of God, that you may be able to withstand in the evil day, and having done all, to stand.

Eternal Father, I reach for you like a child who seeks to be picked up into the arms of his or her loving daddy. Only in your arms am I safe from the evil one. Have I done all, to stand for Christ against the evil day? I'm sure that I have not. Therefore, have pity on me and supply what is lacking in your servant please.

Ephesians 6:14: Stand therefore, having girded your loins with truth, and having put on the breastplate of righteousness,

Jesus, Incarnate Truth, please build me up in the truth that I may stand against my soul's enemy. You, the only Righteous One, be my breastplate, shield and protection in this present spiritual battle. With Incarnate Truth, I can stand, am safe, and able to proclaim the victory that you won on the cross. My only righteousness is your Precious Blood; and because of it, the devil is defeated. Consecrate me in this truth, I beg you.

Ephesians 6:15: and having shod your feet with the equipment of the gospel of peace …

Lord Jesus, the gospel of peace rests in my heart but my feet feel the hot coals of the fire set by the evil one. Teach me please, the way of surrender, strength and suffering wherein I do not lose my peace of soul. Did you lose your peace on the Via Dolorosa? No! You entered into the fiery ordeal with confidence in Your Father's plan. Teach me this way of wise confidence, I beg you. I admit my faith, hope, love are too small. Increase it, I pray.

Scott L. Smith, Jr.

Ephesians 6:16: ... *above all taking the shield of faith, with which you can quench all the flaming darts of the evil one.*

Mother Mary, first disciple of the Lord Jesus, I implore your maternal help to strengthen my faith so it becomes an impenetrable shield. When the flaming darts of the evil one raged against you, they could not mortally wound you. You who were privileged to see God's glory with greatest clarity also saw the unimaginable depths of evil at work all around you. You were not afraid, you believed, and proclaimed God's victory in the greatest battle at the foot of the cross. You stood in valiantly in faith. Please strengthen the faith of your battle worn child now.

Ephesians 6:17: *And take the helmet of salvation, and the sword of the Spirit, which is the word of God.*

Lord Jesus, please renew my mind, that I may think the holy and good thoughts of a redeemed child. Please secure the helmet of salvation upon me so I am never without protection.

Holy Spirit, come and fill me now. Graciously release your gifts of faith, hope and love, discernment and praise. Help me to pick up the sword of the Spirit to cut down and clear away all that is not of you. Keep me rooted in your living Word that is sharper than a two-edged sword against my enemy.

Ephesians 6:18: *Pray at all times in the Spirit, with all prayer and supplication. To that end keep alert with all perseverance, making supplication for all the saints.*

Most Holy Trinity, as a member of your Church militant, I have recourse to the Church triumphant. On earth I can look to, count on, and pray to saints as my heavenly family. In the midst of spiritual battles I have saint friends who passed the test, and their witness strengthens me to fight the good fight. Thank you, my Triune God, for your loving mercy, assurance, protection and blessing.

St. Michael the Archangel, most powerful against Satan and his cohorts, defend me in battle now, and until I am safely home with the Church triumphant. Archangel Michael and beloved guardian angel, please aid me in wearing the full armor of God.

CHAPTER FIVE:
Thirty Bible Verses to Jump Start
Your War Room Prayer Strategy

Old Testament

PSALMS OF DELIVERANCE FROM EVIL AND THANKSGIVING

Psalm 18:1-13, "Royal Thanksgiving for Victory"

> I love thee, O Lord, my strength.
> The Lord is my rock, and my fortress, and my deliverer,
>   my God, my rock, in whom I take refuge,
>   my shield, and the horn of my salvation, my stronghold.
> I call upon the Lord, who is worthy to be praised,
>   and I am saved from my enemies.
> The cords of death encompassed me,
>   the torrents of perdition assailed me;
> the cords of Sheol entangled me,
>   the snares of death confronted me.
> In my distress I called upon the Lord;
>   to my God I cried for help.
> From his temple he heard my voice,
>   and my cry to him reached his ears.

Then the earth reeled and rocked;
   the foundations also of the mountains trembled
   and quaked, because he was angry.
Smoke went up from his nostrils,
   and devouring fire from his mouth;
   glowing coals flamed forth from him.
He bowed the heavens, and came down;
   thick darkness was under his feet.
He rode on a cherub, and flew;
   he came swiftly upon the wings of the wind.
He made darkness his covering around him,
   his canopy thick clouds dark with water.
Out of the brightness before him
   there broke through his clouds
   hailstones and coals of fire.
The Lord also thundered in the heavens,
   and the Most High uttered his voice,
   hailstones and coals of fire.

Psalm 18:31-42,46,48, "Royal Thanksgiving for Victory"

For who is God, but the Lord?
   And who is a rock, except our God?—
the God who girded me with strength,
   and made my way safe.
He made my feet like hinds' feet,
   and set me secure on the heights.
He trains my hands for war,
   so that my arms can bend a bow of bronze.
Thou hast given me the shield of thy salvation,
   and thy right hand supported me,
   and thy help made me great.
Thou didst give a wide place for my steps under me,
   and my feet did not slip.
I pursued my enemies and overtook them;
   and did not turn back till they were consumed.
I thrust them through, so that they were not able to rise;
   they fell under my feet.

For thou didst gird me with strength for the battle;
    thou didst make my assailants sink under me.
Thou didst make my enemies turn their backs to me,
    and those who hated me I destroyed.
They cried for help, but there was none to save,
    they cried to the Lord, but he did not answer them.
I beat them fine as dust before the wind;
    I cast them out like the mire of the streets. [...]
The Lord lives; and blessed be my rock,
    and exalted be the God of my salvation, [...]
who delivered me from my enemies;
    yea, thou didst exalt me above my adversaries;
    thou didst deliver me from men of violence.

Psalm 30:1-5, "Thanksgiving for Recovery from Grave Illness":

I will extol thee, O Lord, for thou hast drawn me up,
    and hast not let my foes rejoice over me.
O Lord my God, I cried to thee for help,
    and thou hast healed me.
O Lord, thou hast brought up my soul from Sheol,
    restored me to life from among those gone down to the Pit.

Sing praises to the Lord, O you his saints,
    and give thanks to his holy name.
For his anger is but for a moment,
    and his favor is for a lifetime.
Weeping may tarry for the night,
    but joy cometh with the morning.

Psalm 34:7-22, "Praise for Deliverance from Trouble":

The angel of the Lord encamps
    around those who fear him, and delivers them.
O taste and see that the Lord is good!
    Happy is the man who takes refuge in him!
O fear the Lord, you his saints,
    for those who fear him have no want!
The young lions suffer want and hunger;

but those who seek the Lord lack no good thing.
Come, O sons, listen to me,
    I will teach you the fear of the Lord.
What man is there who desires life,
    and covets many days, that he may enjoy good?
Keep your tongue from evil,
    and your lips from speaking deceit.
Depart from evil, and do good;
    seek peace, and pursue it.
The eyes of the Lord are toward the righteous,
    and his ears toward their cry.
The face of the Lord is against evildoers,
    to cut off the remembrance of them from the earth.
When the righteous cry for help, the Lord hears,
    and delivers them out of all their troubles.
The Lord is near to the brokenhearted,
    and saves the crushed in spirit.
Many are the afflictions of the righteous;
    but the Lord delivers him out of them all.
He keeps all his bones;
    not one of them is broken.
Evil shall slay the wicked;
    and those who hate the righteous will be condemned.
The Lord redeems the life of his servants;
    none of those who take refuge in him will be condemned.

The Exorcism Psalm - Psalm 91:1-16, "Assurance of God's Protection":

He who dwells in the shelter of the Most High,
    who abides in the shadow of the Almighty,
will say to the Lord, "My refuge and my fortress;
    my God, in whom I trust."
For he will deliver you from the snare of the fowler
    and from the deadly pestilence;
he will cover you with his pinions,
    and under his wings you will find refuge;
    his faithfulness is a shield and buckler.
You will not fear the terror of the night,

nor the arrow that flies by day,
nor the pestilence that stalks in darkness,
    nor the destruction that wastes at noonday.
A thousand may fall at your side,
    ten thousand at your right hand;
    but it will not come near you.
You will only look with your eyes
    and see the recompense of the wicked.
Because you have made the Lord your refuge,
    the Most High your habitation,
no evil shall befall you,
    no scourge come near your tent.
For he will give his angels charge of you
    to guard you in all your ways.
On their hands they will bear you up,
    lest you dash your foot against a stone.
You will tread on the lion and the adder,
    the young lion and the serpent you will trample under foot.
Because he cleaves to me in love, I will deliver him;
    I will protect him, because he knows my name.
When he calls to me, I will answer him;
    I will be with him in trouble,
    I will rescue him and honor him.
With long life I will satisfy him,
    and show him my salvation.

Psalm 138:7-8, "Thanksgiving and Praise":

Though I walk in the midst of trouble,
    thou dost preserve my life;
thou dost stretch out thy hand against the wrath of my enemies,
    and thy right hand delivers me.
The Lord will fulfil his purpose for me;
    thy steadfast love, O Lord, endures forever.
    Do not forsake the work of thy hands.

PROVERBS ON SPIRITUAL WARFARE

Proverbs 5:21-23

For a man's ways are before the eyes of the Lord,
and he watches[e] all his paths.
The iniquities of the wicked ensnare him,
and he is caught in the toils of his sin.
He dies for lack of discipline,
and because of his great folly he is lost.

Proverbs 16:32

He who is slow to anger is better than the mighty,
and he who rules his spirit than he who takes a city.

Proverbs 24:1-12

Be not envious of evil men,
nor desire to be with them;
for their minds devise violence,
and their lips talk of mischief.

By wisdom a house is built,
and by understanding it is established;
by knowledge the rooms are filled
with all precious and pleasant riches.
A wise man is mightier than a strong man,
and a man of knowledge than he who has strength;
for by wise guidance you can wage your war,
and in abundance of counselors there is victory.
Wisdom is too high for a fool;
in the gate he does not open his mouth.
He who plans to do evil
will be called a mischief-maker.
The devising of folly is sin,
and the scoffer is an abomination to men.
If you faint in the day of adversity,
your strength is small.
Rescue those who are being taken away to death;

hold back those who are stumbling to the slaughter.
If you say, "Behold, we did not know this,"
    does not he who weighs the heart perceive it?
Does not he who keeps watch over your soul know it,
    and will he not requite man according to his work?

Proverbs 24:24-27

He who says to the wicked, "You are innocent,"
    will be cursed by peoples, abhorred by nations;
but those who rebuke the wicked will have delight,
    and a good blessing will be upon them.
He who gives a right answer
    kisses the lips.
Prepare your work outside,
    get everything ready for you in the field;
    and after that build your house.

OLD TESTAMENT – OTHER VERSES ON SPIRITUAL WARFARE

Joshua 1:9 – "Have I not commanded you? Be strong and of good courage; be not frightened, neither be dismayed; for the Lord your God is with you wherever you go."

Joshua 23:9-11 – "For the Lord has driven out before you great and strong nations; and as for you, no man has been able to withstand you to this day. One man of you puts to flight a thousand, since it is the Lord your God who fights for you, as he promised you. Take good heed to yourselves, therefore, to love the Lord your God."

Zechariah 3:1-2 – "Then he showed me Joshua the high priest standing before the angel of the Lord, and Satan standing at his right hand to accuse him. And the Lord said to Satan, "The Lord rebuke you, O Satan! The Lord who has chosen Jerusalem rebuke you! Is not this a brand plucked from the fire?"

New Testament

THE GOSPELS ON SPIRITUAL WARFARE

Matthew 6:9-14 – "The Lord's Prayer"

Pray then like this: "Our Father who art in heaven, hallowed be thy name. Thy kingdom come, thy will be done, on earth as it is in heaven. Give us this day our daily bread; and forgive us our debts, as we also have forgiven our debtors; and lead us not into temptation, but deliver us from evil. For if you forgive men their trespasses, your heavenly Father also will forgive you; but if you do not forgive men their trespasses, neither will your Father forgive your trespasses.

Luke 10:17-20 – "The Return of the Seventy"

"The seventy returned with joy, saying, 'Lord, even the demons are subject to us in your name!' And he said to them, 'I saw Satan fall like lightning from heaven. Behold, I have given you authority to tread upon serpents and scorpions, and over all the power of the enemy; and nothing shall hurt you. Nevertheless, do not rejoice in this, that the spirits are subject to you; but rejoice that your names are written in heaven.'"

John 8:31-32 – "Jesus then said to the Jews who had believed in him, 'If you continue in my word, you are truly my disciples, and you will know the truth, and the truth will make you free.'"

John 10:7-11 – "So Jesus again said to them, 'Truly, truly, I say to you, I am the door of the sheep. All who came before me are thieves and robbers; but the sheep did not heed them. I am the door; if any one enters by me, he will be saved, and will go in and out and find pasture. The thief comes only to steal and kill and destroy; I came that they may have life, and have it abundantly. I am the good shepherd. The good shepherd lays down his life for the sheep.'"

John 16:31-33 – "Jesus answered them, 'Do you now believe? The hour is coming, indeed it has come, when you will be scattered, every man to his home, and will leave me alone; yet I am not alone, for the Father is with me. I have said this to you, that in me you may have peace. In the world you have tribulation; but be of good cheer, I have overcome the world.'"

ST. PAUL ON SPIRITUAL WARFARE

One of St. Paul's greatest statements of spiritual warfare occurs in his Letter to the Ephesians, chapter 6. He describes in detail the "Armor of God." This will be discussed in detail, line by line, piece of armor by piece of armor, in a separate chapter.

St. Paul frequently talked about Jesus overcoming the powers of darkness. "According to Your word, Lord, my enemy has been disarmed and embarrassed" (Colossians 2:15).[12] Satan has been "overruled" (Eph 1:20-22), "mastered" (Phil 2:9-11), "rendered powerless" (Heb 2:14), and his works have been "destroyed" (1 John 3:8).

Being these truths into your Prayer War Room. In that stronghold, command the ruin of the darkness with the Truth of Christ.

Romans 8:31-39 – "God's Love in Christ Jesus"

"What then shall we say to this? If God is for us, who is against us? He who did not spare his own Son but gave him up for us all, will he not also give us all things with him? Who shall bring any charge against God's elect? It is God who justifies; who is to condemn? Is it Christ Jesus, who died, yes, who was raised from the dead, who is at the right hand of God, who indeed intercedes for us? Who shall separate us from the love of Christ? Shall tribulation, or distress, or persecution, or famine, or nakedness, or peril, or sword? As it is written,

'For thy sake we are being killed all the day long;
we are regarded as sheep to be slaughtered.'

No, in all these things we are more than conquerors through him who loved us. For I am sure that neither death, nor life, nor angels, nor principalities, nor things present, nor things to come, nor powers, nor height, nor depth, nor anything else in all creation, will be able to separate us from the love of God in Christ Jesus our Lord."

2 Corinthians 10:7-9 – Look at what is before your eyes. If anyone is confident that he is Christ's, let him remind himself that as he is Christ's, so are we. For

---

[12] Also translated as "He disarmed the principalities and powers and made a public example of them, triumphing over them in him" (RSV-CE)

even if I boast a little too much of our authority, which the Lord gave for building you up and not for destroying you, I shall not be put to shame.

Ephesians 1:19-21 – Christ is Made Supreme Over All Things

"… According to the working of his great might which he accomplished in Christ when he raised him from the dead and made him sit at his right hand in the heavenly places, far above all rule and authority and power and dominion, and above every name that is named, not only in this age but also in that which is to come; and he has put all things under his feet and has made him the head over all things for the church, which is his body, the fulness of him who fills all in all."

Philippians 2:9-11 – "Therefore God has highly exalted him and bestowed on him the name which is above every name, that at the name of Jesus every knee should bow, in heaven and on earth and under the earth, and every tongue confess that Jesus Christ is Lord, to the glory of God the Father."

2 Thessalonians 3:1-5 – "Finally, brethren, pray for us, that the word of the Lord may speed on and triumph, as it did among you, and that we may be delivered from wicked and evil men; for not all have faith. But the Lord is faithful; he will strengthen you and guard you from evil. And we have confidence in the Lord about you, that you are doing and will do the things which we command. May the Lord direct your hearts to the love of God and to the steadfastness of Christ."

Hebrews 4:12-13 – "For the word of God is living and active, sharper than any two-edged sword, piercing to the division of soul and spirit, of joints and marrow, and discerning the thoughts and intentions of the heart. And before him no creature is hidden, but all are open and laid bare to the eyes of him with whom we have to do."

Hebrews 11:32-34 – "And what more shall I say? For time would fail me to tell of Gideon, Barak, Samson, Jephthah, of David and Samuel and the prophets— who through faith conquered kingdoms, enforced justice, received promises, stopped the mouths of lions, quenched raging fire, escaped the edge of the sword, won strength out of weakness, became mighty in war, put foreign armies to flight."

Scott L. Smith, Jr.

NEW TESTAMENT – OTHER VERSES ON SPIRITUAL WARFARE

1 Peter 5:8-9 – "Be sober, be watchful. Your adversary the devil prowls around like a roaring lion, seeking someone to devour. Resist him, firm in your faith, knowing that the same experience of suffering is required of your brotherhood throughout the world."

James 4:7-8 – "Submit yourselves therefore to God. Resist the devil and he will flee from you. Draw near to God and he will draw near to you."

Jude v.24-25 – "Benediction"

"Lord, You are able to keep me from stumbling. You will present me blameless in Your presence. It is upon this hope I cast myself and acknowledge Your authority, power, and majesty. To You be all the glory and honor. It is for these things- for Your glory and honor – that I ask Your mighty hand to bring about victory in my life."

REVELATION ON SPIRITUAL WARFARE

Revelation 12: The Woman and the Dragon
The Queen of Heaven

And a great portent appeared in heaven, a woman clothed with the sun, with the moon under her feet, and on her head a crown of twelve stars; she was with child and she cried out in her pangs of birth, in anguish for delivery. And another portent appeared in heaven; behold, a great red dragon, with seven heads and ten horns, and seven diadems upon his heads. His tail swept down a third of the stars of heaven, and cast them to the earth. And the dragon stood before the woman who was about to bear a child, that he might devour her child when she brought it forth; she brought forth a male child, one who is to rule all the nations with a rod of iron, but her child was caught up to God and to his throne, and the woman fled into the wilderness, where she has a place prepared by God, in which to be nourished for one thousand two hundred and sixty days.

Saint Michael Defeats the Dragon

Now war arose in heaven, Michael and his angels fighting against the dragon; and the dragon and his angels fought, but they were defeated and there was no longer any place for them in heaven. And the great dragon was thrown down, that ancient serpent, who is called the Devil and Satan, the deceiver of

46

the whole world—he was thrown down to the earth, and his angels were thrown down with him. And I heard a loud voice in heaven, saying, "Now the salvation and the power and the kingdom of our God and the authority of his Christ have come, for the accuser of our brethren has been thrown down, who accuses them day and night before our God. And they have conquered him by the blood of the Lamb and by the word of their testimony, for they loved not their lives even unto death. Rejoice then, O heaven and you that dwell therein! But woe to you, O earth and sea, for the devil has come down to you in great wrath, because he knows that his time is short!"

The Dragon Fights Again on Earth

And when the dragon saw that he had been thrown down to the earth, he pursued the woman who had borne the male child. But the woman was given the two wings of the great eagle that she might fly from the serpent into the wilderness, to the place where she is to be nourished for a time, and times, and half a time. The serpent poured water like a river out of his mouth after the woman, to sweep her away with the flood. But the earth came to the help of the woman, and the earth opened its mouth and swallowed the river which the dragon had poured from his mouth. Then the dragon was angry with the woman, and went off to make war on the rest of her offspring, on those who keep the commandments of God and bear testimony to Jesus. And he stood on the sand of the sea.

CHAPTER SIX:
Quotes from Holy Men and Women on Spiritual Warfare

Some of the following quotes may be frightening, but I do not include these lightly. It is good to know what we are facing that we may stay "sober and vigilant." Here are a number of great verses to give you the scope of the battle and the wiles of the devil. Let us work to remove the power of the devil's tricks through knowledge of truth.

SAINT FRANCIS OF ASSISI

Not just a garden statue, Francis of Assisi, born Giovanni di Pietro di Bernardone, informally named as Francesco, was an Italian friar, deacon, and preacher. He founded the men's Order of Friars Minor, the women's Order of Saint Clare, the Third Order of Saint Francis and the Custody of the Holy Land.

"By the anxieties and worries of this life Satan tries to dull man's heart and make a dwelling for himself there."

"We should all realize that no matter where or how a man dies, if he is in the state of mortal sin and does not repent, when he could have done so and did not, the Devil tears his soul from his body with such anguish and distress that only a person who has experienced it can appreciate it."

"We need to be especially alert to the evil subtlety of Satan. His one desire is to keep people from having a mind and heart disposed to their Lord and God. . .He wants to extinguish the light of the human heart, and so he moves in by means of worldly busyness and worry."

REVEREND BILLY GRAHAM

Prominent evangelical Christian figure and ordained Southern Baptist minister who gained international renown in the late 1940s.

"We do not war against flesh, but against the demonic realm. For 2 Corinthians 10:3 states, 'For though we walk in the flesh, we do not war after the flesh.'"

"If you are a Christian, you are engaged in a warfare. You're engaged in a battlefield. 'For the weapons of our warfare are not carnal, but mighty through God to the pulling down of strongholds' (2 Corinthians 10:4). The Apostle Paul said, 'I'm going to use some weapons that are going to be new to you, but they are going to pull down the devil's strongholds. And these are spiritual weapons: the word of God and prayer and the power of the Holy Spirit.'"

"Every thought a Christian has should be in obedience to the person of the Lord Jesus Christ. The Apostle Paul tells us that we are to cast 'down imagination and every high thing that exalted itself against the knowledge of God and bring into captivity every thought to the obedience of Christ.'"

"Our thoughts can harm us or help us. Now thoughts are powerful to harm us and powerful to help us. The Bible says, 'As a person thinketh so is it.' How do you think? What goes through your mind? What do you think about when you're alone? [...] One of the most important things in our lives is who is going to control our minds. 'He that ruleth his mind is greater than he that taketh a city' (Proverbs 16:32)."

Scott L. Smith, Jr.

"Our minds are innately against God. Now, the Bible says, first of all, that the mind—your mind—is at enmity against God. Your mind does not want to do anything about God to start with. 'Because the carnal mind is enmity against God: for it is not subject to the law of God, neither indeed can be' (Romans 8:7)."

"The Apostle Paul wrote to the Colossians ... and said that until they had come to Christ, they were alienated and enemies in their mind. Enemies of God, alienated from God, separated from God, in your mind. ... such a mind will not obey the law of God. It submits to sin. It minds the things of the flesh. The Bible warns against having that kind of carnal, fleshly mind. That mind that is dominated by the devil or by selfishness."

"The devil has supernatural power to tempt and blind our minds if we let him. [Satan] has power, supernatural power, to blind your mind. And you let him— you have to let him. And if you let him, he can blind your minds. I cannot account for the apparent veil that hangs over the hearts of some people."

"The only person that can open your eyes to the truth is the Holy Spirit. And you must ask Him to come and open your eyes supernaturally. Which He [can] do tonight ... if you allow Him."

"James says that a double-minded man is unstable in all his ways. And this carries with it the idea of a person who wishes to secure both worlds. You want one foot in heaven and one foot in the pleasures of this life. And you cannot. You've got to go one way or the other."

"Now you cannot help bad thoughts going through your mind. I don't want to give you the wrong impression. ... It's like birds. You can't keep them from flying over, but you don't have to let them nest in your hair. And some of us let evil thoughts nest in our minds."

"The Bibles says ... [to be] transformed by the renewing of your mind. You can be transformed tonight. You can be changed tonight. You can have all of your sins forgiven tonight because Christ died on the cross and shed His blood for you. Have you had your mind renewed and transformed? We are to have the mind of Christ by the transforming and renewing of your mind. You can

50

change your mind and Christ will transform it. That's what repentance really means. We make the commitment to change, He brings the transformation."

SAINT CATHERINE OF SIENA

Catherine was a lay member of the Dominican Order, an Italian mystic, activist, and author, and is considered a Doctor of the Church

"And of what should we be afraid? Our captain on this battlefield is Christ Jesus. We have discovered what we have to do. Christ has bound our enemies for us and weakened them that they cannot overcome us unless we so choose to let them. Therefore, we must fight courageously and mark ourselves with the sign of the most Holy Cross."

FATHER GABRIELLE AMORTH

Chief exorcist of the Diocese of Rome and author of An Exorcist Tells His Story *and* The Antics of Satan and His Army of Fallen Angels

"When I am asked how many demons there are, I answer with the words that the demon himself spoke through a demonic: 'We are so many that, if we were visible, we would darken the sun.'"

"Men are free to choose whether they wish to live for God or against Him and therefore to opt for heaven or for hell. We must recognize that God has made everything to make man happy, and in accordance with this plan, God asks man to obey the laws that He has established; but God has also given man the ability to refuse this truth. This is the situation in which all of us are placed."

"Therefore, it is necessary to guard our heart and our external senses from indecent spectacles: each of us becomes what we see, what we listen to, and what we read."

"The devil, through his ordinary action, which is temptation, and through his extraordinary action, which is the subject of this book, tries to destroy the confidence of each man and each woman to love and to be loved."

On protecting children

"It is necessary to educate them from an early age to cultivate a life of faith through prayer, through the Mass, and through association with the various Catholic youth clubs and other similar organizations. It is absolutely necessary to give them a sense of God and the awareness of the existence of sin and the Devil, the tempter who wishes to lead us to a separation from God and therefore to death. These young people, then, when they become older, will probably have developed the right attitudes toward these sects and satanic practices. I am aware that it involves a difficult form of education, but let us always remember that, because of the total absence of beautiful and good ideals, young people today are more exposed to these dangers. When faith disappears, one abandons himself to superstition and occultism."

"The greatest challenge is normalizing the abnormal and making the extraordinary ordinary."

"The most frequent weak points in man are, from time to time, always the same: pride, money, and lust."

POPE BENEDICT XVI

German pope and significant theologian in his own right

"The more one understands the holiness of God, the more one understands the opposite of what is holy, namely, the deceptive masks of the devil."

"Whatever the less discerning theologians may say, the devil, as far as Christian belief is concerned, is a puzzling but real, personal and not merely symbolical presence. He is a powerful reality (the 'prince of this world,' as he is called by the New Testament, which continually reminds us of his existence), a baneful superhuman freedom directed against God's freedom. This is evident if we look realistically at history, with its abyss of ever-new atrocities which cannot be explained by reference to man alone. On his own, man has not the power to oppose Satan, but the devil is not second to God, and united with Jesus we can be certain of vanquishing him. Christ is 'God Who is near to us,' willing and able to liberate us: that is why the Gospel really is 'Good News.' And that is why we must go on proclaiming Christ in those realms of fear and unfreedom."

POPE SAINT JOHN PAUL II

Polish pope who fought the modernist and communist philosophies of the 20th century

"'Spiritual combat' is another element of life which needs to be taught anew and proposed once more to all Christians today. It is a secret and interior art, an invisible struggle in which (we) engage every day against the temptations, the evil suggestions that the demon tries to plant in (our) hearts."
- *Address of the Holy Father May 25, 2002*

"He who does not believe in the devil does not believe in the Gospel."

"'Begone, Satan!' The Messiah's resolute attitude is an example and an invitation for us to follow him with courageous determination. The devil, the "prince of this world", even today continues his deceitful action. Every man, over and above his own concupiscence and the bad example of others, is also tempted by the devil, and the more so when he is least aware of it."
- *Angelus February 17, 2002*

"Do not be afraid. Do not be satisfied with mediocrity. Put out into the deep and let down your nets for a catch."

"In the inner heart of every person the voice of God and the insidious voice of the Evil One can be heard. The latter seeks to deceive the human person, seducing him with the prospect of false goods, to lead him away from the real good that consists precisely in fulfilling the divine will."
- *Angelus March 9, 2003*

"There is no dignity when the human dimension is eliminated from the person. In short, the problem with pornography is not that it shows too much of the person, but that it shows far too little."

"The great danger for family life, in the midst of any society whose idols are pleasure, comfort and independence, lies in the fact that people close their hearts and become selfish."

"There is no evil to be faced that Christ does not face with us. There is no enemy that Christ has not already conquered. There is no cross to bear that Christ has not already borne for us, and does not now bear with us."

"'Spiritual combat' is another element of monastic life which needs to be taught anew and proposed once more to all Christians today. It is a secret and interior art, an invisible struggle in which monks engage every day against the temptations, the evil suggestions that the demon tries to plant in their hearts; it is a combat that becomes crucifixion in the arena of solitude in the quest for the purity of heart that makes it possible to see God (cf. Matthew 5:8) and of the charity that makes it possible to share in the life of God who is love (cf. 1 John 4:16). More than ever in the lives of Christians today, idols are seductive and temptations unrelenting: the art of spiritual combat, the discernment of spirits, the sharing of one's thoughts with one's spiritual director, the invocation of the Holy Name of Jesus and of his mercy must once more become a part of the inner life of the disciple of the Lord. This battle is necessary in order not to be distracted or worried (cf. 1 Corinthians 7:32,35), and to live in constant recollection with the Lord."

JOHN ECKHARDT

Evangelist and overseer of Crusaders Ministries, located in Chicago, Illinois.

"The Word of God released from your mouth will be planted in your heart. Faith is released from the mouth. The mouth can only release what is in the heart. Faith in the heart that is released through the mouth can move mountains."

- Prayers That Rout Demons: Prayers for Defeating Demons and Overthrowing the Powers of Darkness

Quotes from *Deliverance and Spiritual Warfare Manual: A Comprehensive Guide to Living Free:*

"Jehovah Shalom, You are my peace. You are my prosperity. You're the one who gives me shalom. I refuse to be tormented by the devil, to be vexed, harassed, oppressed, poor, or broke. I refuse to not have the peace of God because Jesus was chastised for my peace. I am a saint of God. I am in covenant. I have a right to peace. I can walk in that covenant. A thousand can fall at my side and ten thousand at my right hand, but it will not come nigh me, because I have a covenant of shalom."

"Hardness of heart prevents us from walking in the fullness of God's blessings."

"Pride hinders people from entering into or walking in covenant. It takes humility to enter in to and walk in covenant."

"Pride always wants to be on top and in control."

POPE FRANCIS

Current pope of the Catholic Church, a Jesuit from Argentina

"The presence of the Devil is on the first page of the Bible, and the Bible ends as well with the presence of the Devil, with the victory of God over the Devil."

"With Eve, 'the father of lies' demonstrates how he is a specialist in tricking people. First, he makes her feel comfortable, then he begins a dialogue with her, leading her 'step by step' where he wants her to go."

"We too are tempted, we too are the target of attacks by the devil because the spirit of Evil does not want our holiness, he does not want our Christian witness, he does not want us to be disciples of Christ. And what does the Spirit of Evil do, through his temptations, to distance us from the path of Jesus? The temptation of the devil has three characteristics and we need to learn about them in order not to fall into the trap. What does Satan do to distance us from the path of Jesus? Firstly, his temptation begins gradually but grows and is always growing. Secondly, it grows and infects another person, it spreads to another and seeks to be part of the community. And in the end, in order to calm the soul, it justifies itself. It grows, it spreads and it justifies itself."

MONSIGNOR LEON CRISTIANI

French priest and author of the twentieth century. His Evidence of Satan in the Modern World *unhesitatingly declares the Devil's existence and activeness, in addition to serving as a solid reference for those studying exorcism and possession.*

"The Devil fears the Virgin Mary more, not only than men and angels but, in a certain sense, than God himself. It is not that the wrath, the power and the hatred of God are not infinitely greater than those of the Blessed Virgin, since Mary's perfections are limited: it is because, in the first place, Satan, being proud, suffers infinitely more from being overcome and punished by the little, humble servant of God, her humility humiliating him more than the divine power; and secondly, because God has given Mary such great power over devils that, as they have often been obliged to admit, in spite of themselves, through the mouths of possessed persons, they are more afraid of one of her sighs of grief over some poor soul, than of the prayers of the saints, and more daunted by a single threat from her than by all their other torments."

ST. PADRE PIO OF PIETRELCINA

Italian friar, priest, stigmatist, and mystic; born Francesco Forgione, he was given the name Pius when he joined the Order of Friars Minor Capuchin.

"The Devil does not want to lose this battle. He takes on many forms. For several days now, he has appeared with his brothers who are armed with batons and pieces of iron. One of the difficulties is that they appear in many disguises. There were several times when they threw me out of my bed and dragged me out of my bedroom. I am patient, however, and I know Jesus, Our Lady, my Guardian Angel, St. Joseph and St. Francis are always with me."

"Prayer is the oxygen of the soul."

"The Spirit of God is a spirit of peace. Even in the most serious faults He makes us feel a sorrow that is tranquil, humble, and confident. This is precisely because of His mercy. The spirit of the devil, instead, excites, exasperates, and makes us feel, in that very sorrow, anger against ourselves. We should, on the contrary, be charitable with ourselves first and foremost. Therefore, if any thought agitates you, this agitation never comes from God, who gives you peace, being the spirit of peace, but from the devil."

"Jesus permits the spiritual combat as a purification, not as a punishment. The trial is not unto death but unto salvation."

"The strength of Satan, who is fighting me, is terrible, but God be praised, because He has put the problem of my health and a victorious outcome into the hands of our heavenly Mother. Protected and guided by such a tender Mother, I will keep on fighting as long as God wishes."

"Pray, hope, and don't worry. Worry is useless. God is merciful and will hear your prayer."

"The evil spirits, because of their pride, anger, and envy, will attempt to turn your gaze away from God through either temptations or harassments. They seek to surround you with their temptations and harassments so that every thought and action you engage in might be in opposition to what the Lord desires for you."

"Do not listen or pay any attention to what the enemy suggests to you, telling you that God has rejected you, or that because of some hidden failure, God is punishing you and wants to chastise you until you eliminate those things from your soul. This is by no means true."

"Calm the tormenting anxieties of your heart, and banish from your imagination all those distressing thoughts and sentiments which are all suggested by Satan in order to make you act badly."

SAINT TERESA OF AVILA

Teresa of Ávila, born Teresa Sánchez de Cepeda y Ahumada, also called Saint Teresa of Jesus, was a Spanish noblewoman who felt called to monastic life.

"May it please His Majesty that we fear Him whom we ought to fear, and understand that one venial sin can do us more harm than all hell together; for that is the truth. The evil spirits keep us in terror, because we expose ourselves to the assaults of terror by our attachments to honours, possessions, and pleasures."

"I feared them [the demons] so little, that the terrors, which until now oppressed me, quitted me altogether; and though I saw them occasionally, — I shall speak of this by and by, — I was never again afraid of them — on the contrary, they seemed to be afraid of me. I found myself endowed with a certain authority over them, given me by the Lord of all, so that I cared no more for them than for flies. They seem to be such cowards; for their strength fails them at the sight of any one who despises them. These enemies have not the courage to assail any but those whom they see ready to give in to them, or when God permits them to do so, for the greater good of His servants, whom they may try and torment."

"But if, for the love of God, we hated all this, and embraced the cross, and set about His service in earnest, Satan would fly away before such realities, as from the plague. He is the friend of lies, and a lie himself. He will have nothing to do with those who walk in the truth."

"From long experience I have learned that there is nothing like holy water to put devils to flight and prevent them from coming back again. They also flee from the Cross, but return; so holy water must have great virtue."

SAINT JOHN VIANNEY

Jean-Marie Vianney, commonly known in English as Saint John Vianney, was a French parish priest who is venerated as the patron saint of parish priests.

"Prayer is to our soul what rain is to the soil. Fertilize the soil ever so richly, it will remain barren unless fed by frequent rains."

"How unhappy we are, my children, thus to be the sport of demons. They do whatever they please with us; they suggest to us evil speaking, calumny, hatred, vengeance; they even drive us so far as to put our neighbor to death."

"The devil only tempts those souls that wish to abandon sin and those that are in a state of grace. The others belong to him; he has no need to tempt them."

"The greatest of all evils is not to be tempted, because there are then grounds for believing that the devil looks upon us as his property."

"I tell you that you have less to suffer in following the cross than in serving the world and its pleasures."

"My friend, the devil is not greatly afraid of the discipline and other instruments of penance. That which beats him is the curtailment of one's food, drink and sleep. There is nothing the devil fears more, consequently, nothing is more pleasing to God. Oh! How often have I experienced it! Whilst I was alone – and I was alone during eight or nine years, and therefore quite free to yield to my attraction – it happened at times that I refrained from food for entire days. On those occasions I obtained, both for myself and for others, whatsoever I asked of Almighty God."

"If Our Lord was tempted, it was in order to show us that we must be also. It follows, therefore, that we must expect temptation. If you ask me what is the cause of our temptations, I shall tell you that it is the beauty and the great worth and importance of our souls which the Devil values and which he loves so much that he would consent to suffer two Hells, if necessary, if by so doing he could drag our souls into Hell."

"When we are tempted by pride, we must immediately humble and abase ourselves before God. If we are tempted against the holy virtue of purity, we must try to mortify our bodies and all our senses and to be ever more vigilant of ourselves. If our temptation consists in a distaste for prayers, we must say even more prayers, with greater attention, and the more the Devil prompts us to give them up, the more we must increase their number."

"Whom does the devil pursue most? Perhaps you are thinking that it must be those who are tempted most; these would undoubtedly be the habitual drunkards, the scandalmongers, the immodest and shameless people who wallow in moral filth, and the miser, who hoards in all sorts of ways. No, my dear brethren, no, it is not these people. On the contrary, the Devil despises them, or else he holds onto them, lest they not have a long enough time in which to do evil, because the longer they live, the more their bad example will drag souls into Hell."

"So, you will ask me, who then are the people most tempted? They are these, my friends; note them carefully. The people most tempted are those who are ready, with the grace of God, to sacrifice everything for the salvation of their poor souls, who renounce all those things which most people eagerly seek. It is not one devil only who tempts them, but millions seek to entrap them."

"The greatest of all evils is not to be tempted because there are then grounds for believing that the Devil looks upon us as his property and that he is only awaiting our deaths to drag us into Hell. Nothing could be easier to understand. Just consider the Christian who is trying, even in a small way, to save his soul. Everything around him inclines him to evil; he can hardly lift his eyes without being tempted, in spite of all his prayers and penances. And yet a hardened sinner, who for the past twenty years has been wallowing in sin, will tell you that he is not tempted! So much the worse, my friend, so much the worse! That is precisely what should make you tremble-that you do not know what temptations arc. For to say that you are not tempted is like saying the Devil no longer exists or that he has lost all his rage against Christian souls. "If you have no temptations," St. Gregory tells us, "it is because the devils are your friends, your leaders, and your shepherds. And by allowing you to pass your poor life tranquilly, to the end of your days, they will drag you down into the depths." St. Augustine tells us that the greatest temptation is not to have temptations because this means that one is a person who has been rejected, abandoned by God, and left entirely in the grip of one's own passions."

SAINT LOUIS DE MONTFORT

Louis-Marie Grignion de Montfort was a French priest and Confessor. He was known in his time as a preacher and was made a missionary apostolic by Pope Clement XI.

"Even if you are on the brink of damnation, even if you have one foot in hell, even if you have sold your soul to the devil as sorcerers do who practice black magic, and even if you are heretic as obstinate as a devil, sooner or later you will be converted and will amend your life and save your soul, if - and mark well what I say - if you say the Rosary devoutly every day until death for the purpose of knowing the truth and obtaining contrition and pardon for your sins."

"The Hail Mary, the Rosary, is the prayer and the infallible touchstone by which I can tell those who are led by the Spirit of God from those who are deceived by the devil. I have known souls who seemed to soar like eagles to the heights by their sublime contemplation and yet were pitifully led astray by the devil. I only found out how wrong they were when I learned that they scorned the Hail Mary and the Rosary, which they considered as being far beneath them. The Hail Mary is a blessed dew that falls from heaven upon the souls of the predestinate. It gives them a marvelous spiritual fertility so that they can grow in all

61

Scott L. Smith, Jr.

virtues. The more the garden of the soul is watered by this prayer, the more enlightened in mind we become, the more zealous in heart, the stronger against all our enemies. The Hail Mary is a sharp and flaming shaft which, joined to the Word of God, gives the preacher the strength to pierce, move, and convert the most hardened hearts, even if he has little or no natural gift for preaching."

REVELATION OF JESUS TO SAINT BRIDGET OF SWEDEN

Venerated by Lutherans, Anglicans, and Catholics, Bridget was a mystic and, though not royalty, is known as the Princess of Nericia

"My enemy has three demons within him. The first resides in his genitals, the second in his heart, the third in his mouth. The first is like a seaman, who lets water in through the keel, and the water, by increasing gradually, fills up the ship. There is a flood of water then, and the ship sinks. This ship stands for his body that is assailed by the temptations of demons and by his own lusts as though by storms. Lust entered first through the keel, that is, through the delight he took in bad thoughts. Since he did not resist through penance or fill the holes with the nails of abstinence, the water of lust grew day by day through his consenting. The ship being then replete or filled with the concupiscence of the belly, the water flooded and engulfed the ship in lust so that he was unable to reach the port of salvation. The second demon, residing in his heart, is like a worm lying in an apple that first eats the apple's core, and then, after leaving its excrements there, roams around inside the apple until the whole apple is ruined. This is what the devil does. First he spoils a person's will and good desires, which are like the core where all the mind's strength and goodness are found, and, once the heart has been emptied of these goods, then he puts in their place in the heart the worldly thoughts and affections that the person had loved more. He then impels the body itself toward his pleasure and, for this reason, the man's courage and understanding diminish and his life becomes tedious. He is indeed an apple without a core, that is, a man without a heart, since he enters my church without a heart, because he has no charity. The third demon is like an archer who, looking around through the windows, shoots the unwary. How can the devil not be in a man who is always including him in his conversation? That which is loved more is more frequently mentioned. The harsh words by which he wounds others are like arrows shot through as many windows as the number of times he mentions the devil or as many times as his words wound innocent people and scandalize simple folk. I who am the truth swear by my truth that I shall condemn him like a whore to fire and brimstone, like an insidious traitor to the mutilation of his limbs, like a scoffer of the Lord to perpetual shame. However, as long as his soul and body are still united, my mercy is open to him. What I require of him is to attend the divine services more frequently, not to be afraid of any reproach or desire any honor and never to have that sinister name on his lips again."

SAINT JOHN BOSCO

John Melchior Bosco, popularly known as "Don Bosco," was an Italian priest, educator, and writer of the 19th century.

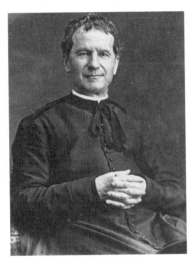

"When tempted, invoke your angel. Ignore the devil and do not be afraid of him. He trembles and flees at your guardian angel's sight."

"Do you want to outwit the devil? Never let him catch you idle. Work, study, pray, and you will surely overcome your spiritual enemy."

"The usual snare with which the devil catches the young is to fill them with shame when they are about to confess their sins. When he pushes them to commit sins, he removes all shame, as if there were nothing wrong with it, but when they are going to confession, he returns that shame magnified and tries to convince them that the priest will be shocked by their sins and will no longer think well of them. Thus, the devil tries to drive souls to the brink of eternal damnation. Oh, how many lads does Satan steal from God — sometimes forever — by this trick."

Scott L. Smith, Jr.

SAINT THOMAS MORE

Celebrate lawyer, jurist, and eventual chancellor of England, whose one-time friend Henry VIII beheaded for his refusal to assent to the king's divorce.

The Devil never runs upon a man to seize him with his claws until he sees him on the ground, already having fallen by his own will.

SAINT IGNATIUS OF LOYOLA

Spanish Basque priest and theologian, the founder of the order of priests called the Society of Jesus, better known as the Jesuits

"The strategy of our adversary can be compared to the tactics of a commander intent upon seizing and plundering a position he desires. The leader of an army will encamp, explore the fortifications and defenses of the fortress, and attack at the weakest point."

"After you have made a decision that is pleasing to God, the devil may try to make you have second thoughts. Intensify your prayer time, meditation, and good deeds. For if Satan's temptations merely cause you to increase your efforts to grow in holiness, he'll have an incentive to leave you alone."

SERVANT OF GOD SOLANUS CASEY

In his extraordinary love, trust, faith, and confidence in God, he became widely known as "Detroit's miracle worker."

"In my opinion, there is hardly anything else that the enemy of our soul dreads more than confidence, humble confidence in God. Confidence in God is the very soul of prayer."

ST. MAXIMILIAN KOLBE

A Polish Franciscan friar, executed by the Nazis at Auschwitz, who has become known as the "Apostle of Consecration to Mary"

"In the face of such strong attacks by the enemies of the Church of God, are we to remain inactive?

64

Is that all we can do, complain and cry? NO! Every one of us has a holy obligation to build a trench and personally hurl back the assaults of the enemy."

SAINT FAUSTINA KOWALSKA

Polish nun and mystic, whose apparitions of Jesus Christ inspired the devotion to the Divine Mercy and earned her the title of "Secretary of Divine Mercy"

Jesus, Himself, began instructing Faustina, "My daughter, I want to teach you about spiritual warfare" and **Jesus provided the following rules for Spiritual Combat:**

"Never trust in yourself but abandon yourself totally to My will."

"In desolation, darkness and various doubts, have recourse to Me and to your spiritual director. He will always answer you in my name."

"Do not bargain with any temptation; lock yourself immediately in My Heart."

"At the first opportunity, reveal the temptation to the confessor."

"Put your self-love in the last place, so that it does not taint your deeds."

"Bear with yourself with great patience."

"Do not neglect interior mortifications."

"Always justify to yourself the opinions of your superiors and of your confessor."

"Shun murmurs like a plague."

"Let all act as they like; you are to act, as I want you to."

Scott L. Smith, Jr.

"Observe the Rule as faithfully as you can." [meaning the "rule" of religious life, like the "Rule of St. Benedict"]

"If someone causes you trouble, think what good you can do for the person who caused you to suffer."

"Do not pour out your feelings."

"Be silent when you are rebuked."

"Do not ask everyone's opinion, but only the opinion of your confessor; be as frank and simple as a child with him."

"Do not become discouraged by ingratitude."

"Do not examine with curiosity the roads down which I lead you."

"When boredom and discouragement beat against your heart, run away from yourself and hide in My heart."

"Do not fear struggle; courage itself often intimidates temptations, and they dare not attack us."

"Always fight with the deep conviction that I am with you."

"Do not be guided by feeling, because it is not always under your control; but all merit lies in the will."

"Always depend upon your superiors, even in the smallest things." [meaning the "superiors" of religious life. Nevertheless, Jesus is always our Lord and superior.]

"I will not delude you with prospects of peace and consolations; on the contrary, prepare for great battles."

"Know that you are on a great stage where all heaven and earth are watching you."

"Fight like a knight, so I can reward you. Do not be unduly fearful, because you are not alone."

St. Therese of Lisieux

Known as the "Little Flower", Saint Thérèse was a French Discalced Carmelite nun known for her "Little Way" spirituality of radical humility before Jesus and who died very young

"I remember a dream I had at that age which impressed itself very deeply on my memory. I thought I was walking alone in the garden when, suddenly, I saw near the arbor two hideous little devils dancing with surprising agility on a barrel of lime, in spite of the heavy irons attached to their feet. At first they cast fiery glances at me; then, as though suddenly terrified, I saw them, in the twinkling of an eye, throw themselves down to the bottom of the barrel, from which they came out somehow, only to run and hide themselves in the laundry which opened into the garden. Finding them such cowards, I wanted to know what they were going to do, and, overcoming my fears, I went to the window. The wretched little creatures were there, running about on the tables, not knowing how to hide themselves from my gaze. From time to time they came nearer, peering through the windows with an uneasy air, then, seeing that I was still there, they began to run about again looking quite desperate. Of course, this dream was nothing extraordinary; yet I think Our Lord made use of it to show me that a soul in the state of grace has nothing to fear from the devil, who is a coward, and will even fly from the gaze of a little child."

CHAPTER SEVEN:
Most Powerful Prayers for Spiritual Warfare

PRAYER OF ST. MICHAEL

St. Michael the Archangel, defend us in battle. Be our defense against the wickedness and snares of the Devil. May God rebuke him, we humbly pray, and do thou, O Prince of the heavenly hosts, by the power of God, thrust into hell Satan, and all the evil spirits, who prowl about the world seeking the ruin of souls. Amen.

PRAYER OF SAINT ALFRED FOR STRENGTH AND GUIDANCE (9TH CENTURY)

Lord God Almighty, shaper and ruler of all creatures, we pray for your great mercy, that you guide us towards you, for we cannot find our way. And guide us to your will, to the need of our soul, for we cannot do it ourselves. And make our mind steadfast in your will and aware of our soul's need.

Strengthen us against the temptations of the devil, and remove from us all lust and every unrighteousness, and shield us against our foes, seen and unseen. Teach us to do your will, that we may inwardly love you before all things with a pure mind. For you are our maker and our redeemer, our help, our comfort, our trust, our hope; praise and glory be to you now and forever. Amen.

PRAYER OF THE BLESSED VIRGIN MARY, QUEEN OF HEAVEN, QUEEN OF ANGELS

August Queen of Heaven, sovereign Mistress of the Angels, who didst receive from the beginning the mission and the power to crush the serpent's head, we beseech thee to send forth thy holy angels, that under thy command and by thy power, they may pursue the evil spirits, encounter them on every side, resist their bold attacks, and drive them hence into the abyss of woe.

Most Holy Mother, send thy angels to defend us and to drive the cruel enemy from us.

All ye holy angels and archangels, help and defend us. Amen.

PRAYER FOR STRENGTH AGAINST SIN

From the Gregorian Sacramentary, a 10th-century illuminated Latin manuscript containing a sacramentary, a book used for the Mass and other liturgies

O God, in wonderful ways you created and redeemed mankind. Give us steadfast minds to resist the allurements of sin that we may attain the joys of eternal life. Hear us, O Lord. Amen.

PRAYER FOR DIVINE HELP AND PROTECTION

From the Liturgy of the Greek Church[13]

You are our helper, Mighty One. and you are no respecter of persons. Help all your people bought with the precious blood of Christ.

You are our fortress and defender. No one can snatch us from your hand. There is no other God like you. In you we trust. Sanctify us through your truth. Your Word is truth.

Preserve us and all your people from injury and deceit, from fear of the enemy, from the arrow that flies by day, and the trouble that walks in the darkness, and grant us eternal life in Christ, your Son, our Lord and Savior. Amen.

---

[13] Wilbur Patterson Thirkield, ed., *Service and Prayers for Church and Home* (1918)

Scott L. Smith, Jr.

PRAYERS FROM VEIT DIETRICH

From Veit Dietrich (d. 1549), a German Lutheran theologian[14]

"Make Us Watchful and Heedful"
>Lord God, heavenly Father,
>make us watchful and heedful
>in awaiting the coming of your Son,
>our Lord Jesus Christ,
>that when he stands at the door and knocks,
>he may find us not sleeping in carelessness and sin,
>but awake and rejoicing in his appearing;
>through your beloved Son,
>Jesus Christ our Lord,
>who lives and reigns with you and the Holy Spirit,
>one true God, now and forever.

"By Your Word You Have Brought Us out of Darkness"
>Lord God, heavenly Father,
>we most heartily thank you
>that by your Word
>you have brought us out of the darkness of error
>into the light of your grace.
>Mercifully help us to walk in that light,
>guard us from all error and false doctrine
>and grant that we may not become ungrateful
>and despise and persecute your Word,
>as your people did long ago,
>but receive it with all our heart,
>govern our lives according to it
>and put all our trust in your grace
>through the merit of your dear Son,
>Jesus Christ our Lord,
>who lives and reigns with you and the Holy Spirit,
>one true God, now and forever.

---

[14] Veit Dietrich, *The Collects of Veit Dietrich in Contemporary English* (2016), Paul C. Stratman, translator.

"We Seek Our Comfort Only in Your Mercy"

Lord God, heavenly Father,
guide and direct us by your Holy Spirit,
that we may not forget our sins and be filled with pride,
but continue in daily repentance and renewal,
seeking our comfort only
in the blessed knowledge
that you will be merciful to us,
forgive us our sins
and grant us eternal life;
through your beloved Son,
Jesus Christ our Lord,
who lives and reigns with you and the Holy Spirit,
one God, now and forever.

"Deliver Us from Eternal Death"

Lord God, heavenly Father,
you sent your Son to be made flesh,
that by his death he might atone for our sins
and deliver us from eternal death.
Confirm in our hearts
the hope that our dear Lord Christ, who
raised the widow's son with a word,
will raise us on the last day
and give us eternal life;
through your beloved Son, Jesus Christ our Lord,
who lives and reigns with you and the Holy Spirit,
one true God, now and forever.

Scott L. Smith, Jr.

PRAYER FOR LIGHT AND GUIDANCE

Leonine Sacramentary, 5ᵗʰ Century

O Lord, enlighten our hearts by your holy radiance, Jesus Christ, that we may serve you without fear in holiness and righteousness all the days of our life.

In him may we survive the storms of this world, and by his guidance reach the country of eternal brightness; through your mercy, O blessed Lord, you live and govern all things, now and forever. Amen.

"MY HOPE AND MY REFUGE" PRAYER FROM THOMAS à KEMPIS

Thomas à Kempis, author of The Imitation of Christ

Ah, Lord God, holy lover of my soul, when you come into my soul, all that is within me will rejoice.

You are my glory and the exultation of my heart. You are my hope and refuge in the day of my trouble. Set me free from all evil passions, and heal my heart of all inordinate affections, cure and cleanse me within, that I may be made fit to love, courageous to suffer, steady to persevere.

Nothing is sweeter than love, nothing more courageous, nothing fuller nor better in heaven and earth; because love is born of God, and cannot rest but in God, above all created things. Let me love you more than myself, and love myself except for you; and in you all that truly love you, as the law of love commands, shining out from yourself.

DAILY DECLARATIONS FROM PASTOR JOHN ECKHARDT

Excerpts from Daily Declarations for Spiritual Warfare: Biblical Principles to Defeat the Devil:

I will cause you to dwell in safety. I have sent my angels to surround you and to cause you to dwell in safety. They will deliver you from all danger and will surround you with My protection. I will hold you up, and you will be safe. My eyes are turned on My righteous servants, and My ears are attentive to your cry. I will deliver you from all your troubles. The name of My Son is a fortified tower for you, and you can run to it where you will be safe. Do not be afraid, for I will guide you safely wherever you go. You can lie down and sleep, for I have made you to dwell in safety. I am Your God, and I will keep you safe and will protect you forever from the wicked who freely strut around in wickedness.

PSALMS 34:7–22; 78:52; 12:5

Prayer Declaration: You will answer me, Lord, when I call to You, and will give me relief from my distress. You will have mercy on me and hear my prayer. You will grant peace in my family, in my land, and no one will cause me to be afraid. You will walk with me and will be My God, and I will be Your faithful servant.

I will enlarge each part of your life. I will break off of your life any limitations and restrictions placed on your life by any evil spirit. I will enlarge each part of your life and will keep you from evil. My kingdom and government will increase in your life, and you will receive deliverance and enlargement for your life. I will let you increase exceedingly. You will increase in wisdom and stature and in strength. You will confound your adversaries as My grace and favor increase in your life. My Word will increase in your life, and the years of your life will be increased. You will flourish like a palm tree and grow like a cedar in Lebanon. They will take root in your house and will do well. They will be trees that stay healthy and fruitful to all your generations.

ISAIAH 9:7; 60:4–5; ACTS 9:22; PSALM 92:12

Prayer Declaration: Cast out my enemies, and enlarge my borders. Enlarge my heart so I can run the way of Your commandments. Enlarge my steps so I can receive Your wealth and prosperity. Let me increase in the knowledge of God, and let me increase and abound in love.

You will overcome the devil by the blood of my Son just as the blood of a lamb, sprinkled on the doorposts in Egypt by My chosen people, established a covenant of blood with Me and protected them from the destruction that I brought to those who had enslaved them, so too have I established a covenant of blood with you. Through the blood of My dear Son, Jesus, which covers you, I have redeemed you from the curse of sin and have adopted you as My own dear child. I have equipped you with everything good for doing My will, and I will work in you to cause you to do what is pleasing to Me. Through the blood of Christ you can have confidence to come into My presence. In His blood, I have given you redemption, forgiveness of sins, and have redeemed you from the power of evil.

EXODUS 12; HEBREWS 13:20–21; REVELATION 12:10–11

Scott L. Smith, Jr.

Prayer Declaration: I have eternal redemption through the power of the blood of Christ. I have been raised to new life in Christ so that I may serve the living God. I overcome the devil through the blood of Jesus. Through Him I am made perfect and have the confidence to enter into the presence of God."

My Truth will remove every false ministry in high places my child, be aware that in these days there are false teachers among you who will secretly bring in destructive heresies, even denying the Lord who saved them, and will cause many to reject My teachings and My way of truth. Their judgment has been idle for a long time, and because they have grown cold to the truth, they will bring on themselves—and others—My swift destruction. Do not listen to their lies, and reject their teachings. They must be removed from their lofty seats of comfort, and the results of their disobedience will become an example to any who might be swayed to follow their ways. Rise up like my servant Josiah, and stand for Me in truth, leading all who know you to turn from evil and to do what is right in My eyes, not turning aside to the right or to the left.
2 PETER 2:1–3; 2 KINGS 22:1–2

Prayer Declaration: Lord, remove every false ministry and strange god from the high places. Let righteous men with Your wisdom sit in the high governmental places of my city and nation. Let the spiritual foundations that were built in my city, community, and nation be restored. Use me to walk in the spirit of Josiah and lead the people into righteousness."

I have broken Leviathan's power from your life, my child. I have broken the demonic power of the sea serpent from your life. I have caused all his demonic little demon fish to stick to his scales as I brought him up out of the midst of the sea and cast him into the wilderness to lie on the open field as food for all the beasts of the field and the birds of the heavens. The rivers and seas belong to Me, and I will make utterly waste and desolate the places where his evil power has dwelt. I am the one who commands the sea and its streams to run dry, and I have broken the power of the evils of the sea from bringing destruction to your life.
EZEKIEL 29:3–5; ISAIAH 44:27

Prayer Declaration: Father, in the name of Jesus I bind every sea monster that would attack my life or region. You have raised a watch against Leviathan, and You will not let the demonic powers of the sea oppress me. You have stripped him of his power and have taken away his armor. You have caused the places of his domain to become utterly waste and desolate and have thrown him and his demonic spirits into the wilderness to be food for the beasts and birds who dwell there.

My precious child, you do not need to be filled with terror and fear when your enemies plot against you and pursue you. Trust instead in Me, for indeed I am Your God, and your times are indeed in My hands. In the shelter of My presence you are hidden from your enemies and from the intrigues of evil men. Do not be afraid of your enemies. I have given them into your hand. Not one of them will be able to withstand you. But don't stop—pursue your enemies. Attack them from the rear, for I, the Lord your God, have given them into your hand. I will remove your enemies from your land just as I would remove savage beasts, and the sword will not pass through your country.
PSALM 31:14–15, 20; JOSHUA 10:8, 19; LEVITICUS 26:6–8
Prayer Declaration: I trust You, Lord. I celebrate and shout because You are kind. You saw all my suffering, and You cared for me. You kept me from the hands of my enemies, and You set me free. I will praise You, Lord, for showing great kindness when I was like a city under attack. You answered my prayer when I shouted for help.

I will destroy the works of lust and perversion, my child. Don't be fooled. Anyone who keeps on sinning belongs to the devil. He has sinned from the beginning, but My Son came to destroy all that he has done. If anyone loves the world, My love is not in him. For all that is in the world—the lust of the flesh, the lust of the eyes, and the pride of life—is not of Me, but is of the world. The world is passing away, and the lust of it. When you ask why the land perishes and burns up like a wilderness so that no one can pass through, I will respond: Because you have forsaken My law which I set before you, and have not obeyed My voice, nor walked according to it. Therefore, I will scatter those who do the works of lust and perversion and will send a sword after them until I have consumed them.
GENESIS 19:12–13; 1 JOHN 2:16; JEREMIAH 9:12–16
Prayer Declaration: Let the spirits of lust and perversion be destroyed with Your fire. Pass through the land and burn up all wickedness and perversion from out of it. The world is passing away, and the lust of it, but he who does the will of God abides forever.

CHAPTER EIGHT:
THE CLASSIC ON
SPIRITUAL WARFARE –
Excerpts from
The Spiritual Combat
by Dom Lorenzo Scupoli

I: Of the Essence of Christian Perfection - Of the Struggle Requisite for its Attainment - And of the Four Things Needful in this Conflict

Would you attain in Christ the height of perfection, and by a nearer and nearer approach to God become one spirit with Him? Before undertaking this greatest and noblest of all imaginable enterprises, you must first learn what constitutes the true and perfect spiritual life. For many have made it to consist exclusively in austerities, maceration of the flesh, hair-shirts, disciplines, long vigils and fasts, and other like bodily hardships and penances. Others, especially women, fancy they have made great progress therein, if they say many vocal prayers, hear many Masses and long Offices, frequent many churches, receive many communions. Others (and those sometimes among cloistered religious) are persuaded that perfection depends wholly upon punctual attendance in choir, upon silence, solitude, and regularity. And thus, some in these, others in various similar actions, suppose that the foundations of perfection may be laid.

But it is not so indeed; for as some of these are means to ac-quire grace, others fruits of grace, they cannot be held to constitute Christian perfection and the true life of grace. They are unquestionably most powerful means, in the hands of those who use them well and discreetly, of acquiring grace in order to gain strength and vigor against their own sinfulness and weak-ness, to defend themselves against our common enemies, to supply all those spiritual aids so necessary to all the servants of God, and especially to beginners in the spiritual life. Again, they are fruits of grace in truly spiritual persons, who chastise the body because it has o ended its Creator, and in order to keep it low and submissive in His service; who keep silence and live solitary that they may avoid the slightest offense against their Lord, and converse with heaven; who attend divine worship, and give themselves to works of piety; who pray and meditate on the life and passion of our Lord, not from curiosity or sensible pleasure, but that they may know better and more deeply their own sinfulness, and the goodness and mercy of God, enkindle ever more and more within their hearts the love of God and the hatred of themselves, following the Son of God with the Cross upon their shoulders in the way of self-abnegation; who frequent the holy sacraments, to the glory of His Divine Majesty, to unite them- selves more closely with God, and to gain new strength against His enemies.

But these external works, though all most holy in themselves, may yet, by the fault of those who use them as the foundation of their spiritual building, prove a more fatal occasion of ruin than open sins. Such persons leave their hearts unguarded to the mercy of their own inclinations, and exposed to the lurking deceits of the devil, who, seeing them out of the direct road, not only lets them continue these exercises with satisfaction, but leads them in their own vain imagination to expatiate on the delights of paradise, and to fancy themselves to be borne aloft amidst the angelic choir and to feel God within them. Some-times they find themselves absorbed in high, or mysterious, and ecstatic meditations, and, forgetful of the world and of all that it contains, they believe themselves to be caught up to the third heaven.

But the life and conversation of such Persons prove the depth of the delusion in which they are held, and their great distance from the perfection after which we are inquiring; for in all things, great and small, they desire to be pre-ferred and placed above others; they are wedded to their own opinion, and ob-stinate in their own will; and blind to their own faults, they are busy and diligent observers and critics of the deeds and words of others.

But touch only with a finger their point of honor, a certain vain estimation in which they hold themselves and would have others to hold them, interrupt their stereotyped devotions, and they are disturbed and o ended beyond meas-ure.

And if, to bring them back to the true knowledge of them-selves and of the way of perfection, Almighty God should send them sickness, or sorrow, or per-secution (that touchstone of His servants' loyalty, which never befalls them without His permission or command), then is the unstable foundation of their spiritual edifice discovered, and its interior, all corroded and defaced by pride, laid bare; for they refuse to resign them-selves to the will of God, to acquiesce in His always righteous though mysterious judgments, in all events, whether joyful or sorrowful, which may befall them; neither will they, after the example of His Divine Son in His sufferings and humiliation, abase themselves below all creatures, accounting their persecutors as beloved friends, as instruments of God's goodness, and cooperators with Him in the mortification. perfection, and salvation of their souls.

Hence it is most certain that such persons are in serious danger; for, the inward eye being darkened, wherewith they con- template themselves and these their external good works, they attribute to themselves a very high degree of perfection; and thus puffed up with pride they pass judgment upon others, while a very extraordinary degree of God's assisting grace is needed to convert themselves. For the open sinner is more easily converted and restored to God than the man who shrouds himself under the cloak of seeming virtue.

You see, then, very clearly that, as I have said, the spiritual life consists not in these things. It consists in nothing else but the knowledge of the goodness and the greatness of God, and of our nothingness and inclination to all evil; in the love of Him and the hatred of ourselves, in subjection, not to Him alone, but for love of Him, to all His creatures; in entire renunciation of all will of our own and absolute resignation to all His divine pleasure; and furthermore, willing and doing all this purely for the glory of God and solely to please Him, and be-cause He so wills and merits thus to be loved and served.

This is the law of love, impressed by the hand of the Lord Himself upon the hearts of His faithful servants; this is the ab- negation of self which He requires of us; this is His sweet yoke and light burden; this is the obedience to which, by His voice and His example, our Master and Redeemer calls us. In aspiring to such sublime perfection you will have to do continual violence to yourself by a generous conflict with your own will in all things, great or small, until it be wholly annihilated; you must prepare yourself, therefore, for the battle with all readiness of mind; for none but brave warriors shall receive the crown.

This is indeed the hardest of all struggles; for while we strive against self, self is striving against us, and therefore is the victory here most glorious and precious in the sight of God. For if you will set yourself to trample down and exterminate all your unruly appetites, desires, and wishes, even in the smallest and most inconsiderable matters, you will render a greater and more acceptable service to God than if you should discipline yourself to blood, fast more rigorously than hermits or anchorites of old, or convert millions of souls, and yet voluntarily leave even one of these evils alive within you. For although the conversion of souls is no doubt more precious to the Lord than the mortification of a fancy, nevertheless nothing should in your sight be of greater account than to will and to do that very thing which the Lord specially demands and requires of you. And He will infallibly be better pleased that you should watch and labor to mortify your passions than if, consciously and willfully leaving but one alive within you, you should serve Him in some other matter of greater importance in itself.

Now that you see wherein Christian perfection consists, and that it requires a continual sharp warfare against self, you must provide yourself with four most sure and necessary weapons, in order to secure the palm and gain the victory in this spiritual combat.

These weapons are:

- ❖ Distrust of self (diffidence of ourselves);
- ❖ Trust in God (confidence in God);
- ❖ Exercise; and
- ❖ Prayer.

Of all these we will, with the Divine assistance, treat briefly and plainly.

The First Two Weapons
of the Spiritual Combat

II: Distrust of Self (diffidence)

S o necessary is self-distrust in this conflict, that without it you will be unable, I say not to achieve the victory desired, but even to overcome the very least of your passions. And let this be well impressed upon your mind; for our corrupt nature too easily inclines us to a false estimate of ourselves; so that, being really nothing, we account ourselves to be something, and presume, without the slightest foundation, upon our own strength.

This is a fault not easily discerned by us, but very displeasing in the sight of God. For He desires and loves to see in us a frank and true recognition of this most certain truth, that all the virtue and grace which is within us is derived from Him alone, Who is the fountain of all good, and that nothing good can proceed from us, no, not even a thought which can find acceptance in His sight.

And although this very important self-distrust is itself the work of His Divine Hand, and is bestowed upon His beloved, now by means of holy inspirations, now by sharp chastisements and violent and almost irresistible temptations, and by other means which we ourselves do not understand; still it is His will that we on our part should do all in our power to attain it. I therefore set before you four methods, by the use of which, in dependence always on Divine grace, you may acquire this gift.

❖ The first is, to know and consider your own vileness and nothingness, and your inability of yourself to do any good, by which to merit an entrance into the kingdom of heaven.

❖ The second, continually to ask it of the Lord in fervent and humble prayer; for it is His gift. And in order to reach its attainment we must look upon ourselves not only as destitute thereof, but as of ourselves incapable of acquiring it. Present yourself, therefore, continually before the Divine Majesty, with an assured faith that He is willing of His great goodness to grant your petition; wait patiently all the time which His Providence ap-points, and without doubt you shalt obtain it.

❖ The third is, to stand in fear of your own judgment about yourself, of your strong inclination to sin, of the countless hosts of enemies against whom you are incapable of mak-ing the slight- est resistance, of their long practice in open warfare and secret stratagem, of their transformations in-to angels of light, and of the innumerable arts and stares which they secretly spread for us even in the very way of holiness.

❖ The fourth is, whenever you art overtaken by any fault, to look more deeply into yourself, and more keenly feel your absolute and utter weakness; for to this end did God permit your fall, that, warned by His inspiration and illu-mined by a clearer light than before, you may come to know yourself, and learn to despise yourself as a thing unutterably vile, and be therefore also willing to be so accounted and despised by others. For without this willingness there can be no holy self-distrust, which is founded on true humility and experimental self-knowledge.

This self-knowledge is clearly needful to all who desire to be united to the Supreme Light and Uncreated Truth; and the Di-vine Clemency often makes use of the fall of proud and pre-sumptuous men to lead to It; justly suffering them to fall into some faults which they trusted to avoid by their own strength, that they may learn to know and absolutely distrust them-selves.

Our Lord is not, however, wont to use so severe a method, until those more gracious means of which we have before spo-ken have failed to work the cure designed by His Divine Mercy. He permits a man to fall more or less deep-ly in proportion to his pride and self-esteem; so that if there were no presump-tion (as in the case of the Blessed Virgin Mary), there would be no fall. There-fore, whenever you shall fall, take refuge at once in humble self-knowledge, and beseech the Lord with urgent en-treaties to give you light truly to know your-self, and entire self-distrust, lest you should fall again perhaps into deeper perdi-tion.

III: Of Trust in God (confidence)

Self-distrust, necessary as we have shown it to be in this conflict, is not alone sufficient. Unless we would be put to flight, or re-main helpless and vanquished in the hands of our enemies, we must add to it perfect trust in God, and expect from Him alone succor and victory. For as we, who are nothing, can look for nothing from ourselves but falls, and therefore should utterly distrust ourselves; so from our Lord may we assuredly expect complete victory in every conflict. To obtain His help, let us therefore arm ourselves with a lively confidence in Him.

And this also may be accomplished in four ways:

❖ First, by asking it of God.

❖ Secondly, by gazing with the eye of faith at the infinite wisdom and omnipotence of God, to which nothing is impossible or di cult, and con ding in His unbounded goodness and unspeakable willingness to give, hour-by-hour and moment-by-moment, all things needful for the spiritual life, and perfect victory over ourselves, if we will but throw ourselves with confidence into His Arms. For how shall our Divine Shepherd, Who followed after His lost sheep for three-and-thirty years with loud and bitter cries through that painful and thorny way, wherein He spilt His Heart's Blood and laid down His life how shall He refuse to turn His quickening glance upon the poor sheep which now follows Him in obedience to His commands, or with a desire (though sometimes faint and feeble) to obey Him! When it cries to Him piteously for help, will He not hear, and laying it upon His Divine Shoulders, call upon His friends and all the angels of heaven to rejoice with Him? For if our Lord ceased not to search most diligently for the blind and deaf sinner, the lost drachma of the gospel, till He found him; can He abandon him who, like a lost sheep, cries and calls piteously upon his Shepherd? And if God knocks continually at the heart of man, de-siring to enter in and sup there, and to communicate to it His gifts, who can believe that when that heart opens and invites Him to enter, He will turn a deaf ear to the invitation, and refuse to come in?

❖ Thirdly, the third way to acquire this holy confidence is, to call to mind that truth so plainly taught in Holy Scripture, that no one who trusted in God has ever been confounded.

❖ The fourth, which will serve at once towards the attainment of self-distrust and of trust in God, is this: when any duty presents itself to be done, any struggle with self to be made, any victory over self to be at-tempted, before proposing or resolving upon it, think first upon your own weakness; next turn, full of self-distrust, to the wisdom, the power, and the goodness of God; and in reliance upon these, resolve to labor and to fight generously. Then, with these weapons in your hands, and with the help of prayer (of which we shall speak in its proper place), set yourself to labor and to strive.

Unless you observe this order, though you may seem to your-self to be do-ing all things in reliance upon God, you will too often find yourself mistaken; for so common is a presumptuous self-confidence, and so subtle are the forms it assumes, that it lurks almost always even under an imagined self-distrust and fancied confidence in God.

To avoid presumption as much as possible, and in order that all your works may be wrought in distrust of self and trust in God, the consideration of your own weakness must precede the consideration of God's omnipotence; and both together must precede all your actions.

IV: How a man may know whether he is active in Self-Distrust and Trust in God

The presumptuous servant often supposes that he has acquired self-distrust and trust in God when the case is far otherwise.

And this will be made clear to thee by the effect produced on thy mind by a fall. If thou art so saddened and disquieted thereby as to be tempted to despair of making progress or doing good, it is a sure sign that thy trust is in self and not in God. For he who has any large measure of self-distrust and trust in God feels neither surprise, nor despondency, nor bitterness, when he falls; for he knows that this has arisen from his own weakness and want of trust in God. On the contrary, being, rendered thereby more distrustful of self, more humbly con dent in God, detesting above all things his fault and the unruly passions which have occasioned it, and mourning with a quiet, deep, and patient sorrow over his offense against God, he pursues his enterprise, and follows after his enemies, even to the death, with a spirit more resolute and undaunted than before.

I would that these things were well considered by certain persons so called spiritual, who cannot and will not be at rest when they have fallen into any fault.

They rush to their spiritual father, rather to get rid of the anxiety and uneasiness which spring from wounded self-love than for that purpose which should be their chief end in seeking him, to purify themselves from the stain of sin, and to fortify themselves against its power by means of the most Holy Sacrament of Penance.

V: Of the Error of Many, Who Mistake Faint-heartedness for a Virtue

Many also deceive themselves in this way, they mistake the fear and uneasiness which follow after sin for virtuous emotions; and know not that these painful feelings spring from wounded pride, and a presumption which rests upon confidence in themselves and their own strength. They have accounted themselves to be something, and relied unduly upon their own powers. Their fall proves to them the vanity of this self-dependence, and they are immediately troubled and astonished as at some strange thing, and are disheartened at seeing the prop to which they trusted suddenly give way.

This can never befall the humble man, who trusts in his God alone, and in nothing presumes upon himself. Though grieved when he falls into a fault, he is neither surprised nor disquieted; for he knows that his own misery and weakness, already clearly manifest to himself by the light of truth, have brought all this upon him.

VI: Further directions how to attain Self-Distrust and Trust in God

Since our whole power to subdue our enemies arises principally from self-distrust and trust in God, I will give you some further directions to enable you, by the Divine Assistance, to acquire it. Know, then, for a certain truth, that neither all gifts, natural or acquired, nor all graces given gratis, nor the knowledge of all Scripture, nor long habitual exercise in the service of God, will enable us to do His will, unless in every good and acceptable work to be performed, in every temptation to be overcome, in every peril to be avoided, in every Cross to be borne in conformity to His will, our heart be sustained and up-borne by an especial aid from Him, and His hand be outstretched to help us. We must, then, bear this in mind all our life long, every day, every hour, every moment, that we may never indulge so much as a thought of self-confidence.

And as to confidence in God, know that it is as easy to Him to conquer many enemies as few; the old and experienced as the weak and young.

Therefore, we will suppose a soul to be heavy-laden with sins, to have every possible fault and every imaginable defect, and to have tried, by every possible means and every kind of Spiritual Exercise, to forsake sin and to practice holiness. We will suppose this soul to have done all this, and yet to have failed in making the smallest advance in holiness, nay, on the contrary, to have been borne the more strongly towards evil.

For all this she must not lose her trust in God, nor give over her spiritual conflict and lay down her arms, but still fight on resolutely, knowing that none is vanquished in this spiritual com- bat but he who ceases to struggle and loses confidence in God, whose succor never fails His soldiers, though He sometimes permits them to be wounded. Fight on, then, valiantly; for on this depends the whole issue of the strife; for there is a ready and effectual remedy for the wounds of all combatants who look confidently to God and to His aid for help; and when they least expect it they shall see their enemies dead at their feet.

The Third Weapon of the Spiritual Combat

VII: Of Spiritual Exercises and first of the Exercise of the Understanding, which must be kept guarded against ignorance and curiosity

If in this warfare we are provided with no weapons except self-distrust and trust in God, needful as both these are, we shall not only fail to gain the victory over ourselves, but shall fall into many evils. To these, therefore, we must add the use of Spiritual Exercises, the third weapon named above.

And these relate chiefly to the Understanding and the Will. As regards the Understanding, we must guard against two things which are apt to obscure it. One is ignorance, which darkens it and impedes it in acquiring the knowledge of truth, the proper object of the understanding. Therefore, it must be made clear and bright by exercise, that so it may be able to see and discern plainly all that is needful to purify the soul from disorderly passions, and to adorn it with saintly virtues.

This light may be obtained in two ways. The first and most important is prayer, imploring the Holy Ghost to pour it into our hearts. This He will not fail to do, if we in truth seek God alone and the fulfillment of His holy will, and if in all things we submit our Judgment to that of our spiritual father.

The other is, to exercise ourselves continually in a true and deep consideration of all things, to discover whether they be good or evil, according to the teaching of the Holy Ghost, and not according to their outward appearance, as they impress the senses or are judged of by the world.

This consideration, if rightly exercised will teach us to regard as falsehood and vanity all which the blind and corrupt world in so many various ways loves, desires, and seeks after. It will show us plainly that the honors and pleasures of earth are but vanity and vexation of spirit; that injury and infamy inflicted on us by the world bring true glory, and tribulations contentment; that to pardon our enemies and to do them good is true magnanimity, and an act which likens us most nearly to God; that to despise the world is better than to rule it; that voluntary obedience for the love of God to the meanest of His creatures is greater and nobler than to command mighty princes; and that the mortification and subjugation of our most trifling appetite is more glorious than the reduction of strong cities, the defeat of mighty armies, the working of miracles, or the raising of the dead.

VIII: Of the hindrances to a Right Discernment of Things, and of the method to be adopted in order to understand them properly

The cause of our not rightly discerning all these things and many others is, that we conceive a love or hatred of them at first sight. Our understanding is thus darkened, so that it cannot judge of them correctly.

Lest you fall into this delusion, take all possible care to keep your will pure and free from inordinate affection for anything whatsoever.

When any object, then, is presented to you, view it with your understanding; and consider it maturely before you are moved by hatred to reject it, if it be a thing contrary to your inclinations, or by love to desire it, if it be pleasing to them.

For thus the understanding, being unclouded by passion, will be free and clear, and able to perceive the truth, and to discern the evil which lurks behind delusive pleasure and the good which is veiled under the appearance of evil.

But if the will be first inclined to love or hate anything, the understanding will be unable to exercise a right judgment upon it. For the affection which has thus intruded itself so obscures the understanding, that it views the object as other than it is, and by thus representing it to the will, influences that faculty, in contradiction to every law and rule of reason, to love or hate it inordinately. The understanding is gradually darkened more and more, and in this deepening obscurity the object appears more and more hateful or lovely to the will.

Hence, if this most important rule be not observed, these two faculties, the understanding and the will, noble and excellent as they are, will soon sink in a miserable descent from darkness into thicker darkness, and from error into deeper error.

Guard yourself most vigilantly, then, from all inordinate affection for anything whatever, until you have first tested it by the light of the understanding, and chiefly by that of grace and prayer, and by the judgment of your spiritual father.

And this is to be observed most carefully with regard to such outward works as are good and holy, because the danger is greatest here of delusion and indiscretion.

Hence you may here receive serious injury from some circumstance of time, or place, or degree, or regarding obedience; as has been proved by many, who have incurred great danger in the performance of commendable and holy exercises.

IX: Of another danger from which the Understanding must be guarded in order that it may exercise a True Discernment

The second thing from which the understanding must be guarded is curiosity; for by filling it with hurtful, vain, and impertinent thoughts we incapacitate and disable it from apprehending that which most nearly affects our true mortification and perfection. To this end, you must be as one dead to all needless investigation of even lawful earthly things.

Always restrain your intellect as much as possible, and love to keep it low.

Let the news and the changes of the world, whether great or small, be to you as though, they were not; and should they intrude themselves, reject, and drive them from you.

Be sober and humble even in the desire to understand heavenly things, wishing to know nothing but Christ crucified, His life, His death, and what He requires of thee. Cast all other things far from you, and so shall you be very pleasing unto God. For He loves and delights in those who desire and seek of Him such things alone as serve to the love of His divine goodness and the fulfillment of His will. All other petitions and inquiries belong to self-love, pride, and the snares of the devil.

By following these instructions you will avoid many dangers; for when the wily serpent sees the will of those who are aiming at the spiritual life to be strong and resolute, he attacks their understanding, that so he may master both the one and the other.

He often, therefore, infuses lofty and curious speculations into their minds, especially if they be of an acute and intellectual order, and easily inflated with pride; and he does this in order that they may busy themselves in the enjoyment and discussion of such subjects, wherein, as they falsely persuade themselves, they enjoy God, and meanwhile neglect to purify their hearts and to apply themselves to self-knowledge and true mortification. So, falling into the snare of pride, they make an idol of their own understanding.

Hence, being already accustomed to have recourse in all circumstances to their own judgment, they come gradually and imperceptibly to believe that they have no need of advice or control from others.

This is a most perilous case, and very hard to cure, the pride of the understanding being more dangerous than that of the will; for when the pride of the will is once perceived by the understanding, it may in course of time be easily remedied by submission to those to whom it owes obedience. But how, or by whom, can he be cured, who obstinately believes his own opinion to be worth more than that of others? How shall he submit to other men's judgment, which he accounts to be far inferior to his own!

The understanding is the eye of the soul, by which the wound of the proud will should be discovered and cleansed; if that eye, then, itself be weak and blind and swollen with pride, by whom shall it be healed?

And if the light become darkness, and the rule faulty, what will become of the rest?

Therefore, resist this dangerous pride betimes, before it penetrates into the marrow of your bones.

Blunt the acuteness of your intellect, willingly submit your own opinion to that of others, become a fool for the love of God, and you shall be wiser than Solomon.

Scott L. Smith, Jr.

X: Of the Exercise of the Will, and the end to which all our actions, whether Interior or Exterior, should tend

Besides this necessary exercise of the understanding, you must so regulate your will that it may not be left to follow its own desires, but may be in all things conformed to the Divine pleasure.

And remember, that it is not enough only to strive after those things which are most pleasing to God; but you must so will them, and so do them, as moved thereto by Him, and with a view to please Him alone.

In this exercise of the will, even more than in that of the understanding, we shall meet with strong opposition from nature, which seeks itself and its own ease and pleasure in all things; but especially in such as are holy and spiritual. It delights itself in these, feeding greedily upon them as upon wholesome food.

As soon, therefore, as they are presented to us we look wistfully upon them, and desire them, not because such is the will of God, nor with the sole view to please Him, but for the sake of the satisfaction and benefit to be derived from willing those things which God wills.

This delusion is the more subtle from the very excellence of the thing desired. Hence, even in the desire after God Himself, we are exposed to the delusions of self-love, which often leads us to look more to our own interests, and to the benefits we expect from God, than to His will, which is, that we should love, and desire and obey Him for His own glory alone.

I will now show you a way to avoid this way, which would impede you in the path of perfection, and to accustom yourself to will and to do all things as moved by the Spirit of God, and with the pure intention of honoring and pleasing Him alone, Who desires to be the one End and Principle of our every word and action. When anything presents itself to you as if willed by God, do not permit yourself to will it till you have first raised your thoughts to Him to discover whether He wills you to will it, and because He so wills it, and to please Him alone.

Let your will, then, being thus moved and attracted by His, be impelled to will it because He wills it, and solely to please and honor Him.

In like manner, if you would refuse things which are contrary to God's will, refuse them not till you have first fixed the eye of your mind upon His divine will, Who wills that you should refuse them solely to please Him.

Know, however that the frauds and deceits of wily nature are but little suspected; for, ever secretly seeking self, it often leads us to fancy that our end and motive is to please God when in reality it is far otherwise.

Thus, when we choose or refuse anything for our own interest and satisfaction, we often imagine that we are choosing or refusing it in the hope of pleasing, or in the fear of displeasing, God.

The true and effectual remedy for this delusion is purity of heart, which consists in this – which is indeed the aim and object of all this spiritual warfare – the putting off the old man, and the putting on the new.

And to this end, seeing you are full of self, take care in the beginning of every action to free yourself as much as possible from all admixture of anything which seems to be your own.

Choose nothing, do nothing, refuse nothing, unless you first feel yourself moved and drawn thereto by the pure and simple will of God.

If you do not always feel thus actuated in the inward workings of the mind, and in outward actions, which are but transient, you must be content to have this motive ever virtually present, always maintaining a pure intention to please your God alone in all things. But in actions of longer duration it is well not only to excite this motive within yourself at the beginning, but also to renew it frequently, and to keep it alive till the end. Otherwise you will be in danger of falling into another snare of our natural self-love, which, as it is always inclined to yield rather to self than to God, often causes us unconsciously, in the course of time to change our objects and our aims.

The servant of God who is not on his guard against this danger, often begins a work with the single thought of pleasing his Lord alone; but soon, gradually and almost imperceptibly, he be- gins to take such pleasure in his work, that he loses sight of the Divine Will and follows his own. He dwells so much on the satisfaction he feels in what he is doing, and on the honor and benefit to be derived therefrom, that should God Himself place any impediment in the way, either by sickness or accident or through the agency of man, he is immediately troubled and disquieted, and often falls to murmuring against the impediment, whatever it may be, or rather, against God Himself – a clear proof that his intention was not wholly from God, but sprang from an evil root and a corrupted source.

For he who acts only as moved by God, and with a view to please Him alone, desires not one thing above another. He wishes only to have what it pleases God he should have, and at the time and in the way which may be most agreeable to Him; and whether he have it or not, he is equally tranquil and content; because in either case he obtains his wish, and fulfills his intention, which is nothing else but simply to please God.

Therefore, recollect yourself seriously, and be careful always to direct every action to this perfect end.

And although the bent of your natural disposition should move you to do good through fear of the pains of hell or hope of the joys of paradise, you may even here set before you, as your ultimate end, the will and pleasure of God, Who is pleased that you should enter into His kingdom and not into hell. It is not in man fully to apprehend the force and virtue of this motive; for the most insignificant action, done with a view to please God alone, and for His sole glory, is (if we may so speak) of infinitely greater value than many others of the greatest dignity and importance done without this motive. Hence a single penny given to a poor man with the sole desire to please His Divine Majesty, is more acceptable to God than the entire renunciation of all earthly goods for any other end, even for the attainment of the bliss of heaven; an end in itself not only good, but supremely to be desired.

This exercise of doing all things with the single aim to please God alone seems hard at first, but will become plain and easy by practice, if, with the warmest affections of the heart, we desire God alone, and long for Him as our only and most perfect good; Who deserves that all creatures should seek Him for Himself, and serve Him and love Him above all things.

The deeper and more continual our meditations are upon His infinite excellence, the more fervent and the more frequent will be these exercises of the will; and we shall thus acquire more easily and more speedily the habit of performing every action from pure love to that gracious Lord, Who alone is worthy of our reverence and love.

Lastly, in order to the attainment of this divine motive, I advise you to seek it of God by importunate prayer, and to meditate frequently upon the innumerable benefits which He, of His pure and disinterested love, has bestowed upon us.

XI: Of some considerations which may incline the Will to seek to please God in all things

Furthermore, to incline the will more readily to seek God's honor and glory in all things, always remember that, in many and various ways, He has first loved and honored you.

In creation, by creating you out of nothing after His likeness, and all other creatures for your service.

In Redemption, by sending, not an angel, but His only begotten Son, to redeem you, not with the corruptible price of silver and gold, but with His Precious Blood, and by His most painful and ignominious death. Remember, that every hour, nay, every moment, He protects you from your enemies, fights for you by His grace, offers you continually, in the Sacrament of the Altar, His well-beloved Son, to be your food and your defense; are not all these tokens of the inestimable regard and love borne to you by the Infinite God? It is not in man to conceive, on the one hand, how great is the value which so great a Lord sets upon us poor creatures in our loneliness and misery; and, on the other, how great the return we are bound to make to His Supreme Majesty, Who has done so many and such great things for us.

For if earthly lords, when honored even by poor and lowly men, feel bound to honor them in return, how should our vile nature demean itself towards the Supreme King of heaven and earth, by Whom we are so dearly loved and so highly prized?

And besides all this, and before all things, keep ever vividly in mind that the Divine Majesty is infinitely worthy to be loved for Himself alone, and to be served purely for His own good pleasure.

XII: Of the diverse wills in Man, and the Warfare between them

A
lthough in this combat we may be said to have within us two wills, the one of the reason which is called rational and superior, the other of the senses, called sensual and inferior, and commonly described by the words appetite, flesh, sense, and passion; yet, as it is the reason which constitutes us men, we cannot be said to will anything which is willed by the senses unless we be also inclined thereto by the superior will. And herein does our spiritual conflict principally consist. The reasonable will being placed, as it were, midway between the Divine will, which is above it - and the inferior will, or will of the senses, which is beneath it, is continually assaulted by both; each seeking in turn to attract and subdue, and bring it into obedience.

Much hard toil and trouble must, however, be undergone by the unpracticed, especially at the outset, when they resolve to amend their evil lives, and, renouncing the world and the flesh, to give themselves up to the love and service of Jesus Christ. For the opposition encountered by the superior will, from the continual warfare between the Divine and sensual will, is sharp and severe, and accompanied by acute suffering.

It is not so with those who are well practiced in the way of virtue or of vice; they pursue without difficulty the path on which they have entered; the virtuous yielding readily to the Divine will, and the vicious yielding without resistance to the will of the senses.

But let no one imagine it possible to persevere in the exercise of true Christian virtues, or to serve God as He ought to be served, unless he will in good earnest do violence to himself, and endure the pain of parting with all pleasant things whatsoever, whether great or small, around which his earthly affections are entwined.

Hence it is that so few attain to perfection; for after having with much toil overcome the greater vices, they will not persevere in doing violence to themselves by struggling against the promptings of self-will, and an infinity of lesser desires. They grow weary of so unremitting a struggle; they suffer these insignificant enemies to prevail against them, and so to acquire an absolute mastery over their hearts.

To this class belong men who, if they do not take what be- longs to others, cleave with inordinate affection to that which is lawfully their own. If they do not obtain honors by unlawful means, yet they do not, as they should, shun them; but, on the contrary, cease not to desire, and sometimes even to seek, them in various ways. If they observe fasts of obligation, yet they do not mortify their palate in the matter of superfluous eating, or the indulgence in delicate morsels. If they live continently, yet they do not renounce many indulgences which much impede union with God and the growth of the spiritual life; and which, as they are very dangerous even to the holiest persons, and most dangerous to those who fear them least, should be as much as possible avoided by all.

Hence all their good works are performed in a lukewarm spirit, and accompanied by much self-seeking, by many lurking imperfections, by a certain kind of self-esteem, and by a desire to be praised and valued by the world.

Such persons not only fail to make any progress in the way of salvation, but rather go back; and are therefore in danger of relapsing into their former sins, because they have no love of true holiness, and show little gratitude to their Lord, Who rescued them from the tyranny of the devil. They are moreover too blind and ignorant to see the peril in which they stand; and so falsely persuade themselves of their own security.

And here we discover a delusion, which is the more dangerous because it is little apprehended. Many who aspire to the spiritual life, unconsciously love themselves far more than they ought to do; and therefore practice for the most part those exercises which suit their taste, and neglect others, which touch to the quick those natural inclinations and sensual appetites against which they ought in all reason to direct the full strength of the battle.

Therefore, I exhort and counsel you to be in love with pain and difficulty; for they will bring with them that which is the end and object of the whole struggle: victory over-self. The more deeply you shall be in love with the difficulties encountered by beginners in virtue and in war, the surer and the speedier shall be the victory; and if your love be to the difficulty and the toilsome struggle, rather than to the victory and the virtue to be attained, you shall the more speedily obtain all you desire.

XIII: Of the way to resist the impulses of sense, and of the acts to be performed by the will in order to acquire Habits of Virtue

Whenever your reasonable will is attacked by the will of sense on the one hand, and the Divine will on the other, each seeking to obtain the mastery over it, you must make use of various exercises, in order that the Divine will may always govern you.

- ❖ First, whenever you are assailed and buffeted by the impulses of sense, oppose a valiant resistance to them, so that the superior will may not consent.
- ❖ Secondly, when the assaults have ceased, excite them anew, in order to repress them with greater force and vigor. Then challenge them again to a third conflict, wherein you may accustom yourself to repulse them with contempt and abhorrence. These two challenges to battle should be made to every disorderly appetite, except in the case of temptations of the flesh, concerning which we shall speak in their place.
- ❖ Lastly, make acts contrary to each evil passion which is to be resisted.

This will be made clear by the following example.

Suppose you are assailed by feelings of impatience. Look carefully into yourself, and you will find that these feelings are constantly directed against the superior will, in order to win its consent.

Now, then, begin the first exercise; and by repeated acts of the will, do all in your power to stifle each feeling as it arises, that your will may not consent to it. And never desist from this till, wearied unto death, your enemy yield himself vanquished.

But see here the malice of the devil. When he perceives that we resist the first movements of any passion, not only does he desist from exciting them, but when excited, he endeavors for the time to allay them, lest, by the exercise of resistance to the passion, we should acquire the habit of the opposite virtue. He would fain also betray us into the snares of pride and vainglory, by subtly insinuating to us that, like valiant soldiers, we have quickly trampled down our enemies.

Proceed, therefore, to the second conflict, recalling and ex- citing within yourself those thoughts which tempted you to impatience, until they sensibly affect you. Then set yourself to repress every such feeling with a stronger will and more earnest endeavor than before.

And because, however strenuously we have resisted our enemies, from a sense of duty and a desire to please God, we are still in danger, unless we hold them in perfect detestation, of being one day overcome, attack them again even a third time; and repel them, not with repugnance only, but with indignation, until they have become hateful and abominable in your sight.

Lastly, to adorn and perfect your soul in the habit of all the virtues, exercise yourself in the inward sets directly opposed to all your disorderly passions.

Would you attain, for instance, to the perfection of patience? On receiving any insult which tempts you to impatience, it will not be enough to exercise yourself in the three modes of warfare above described, you must do more even willingly accept and love the indignity you have endured; desiring to submit to it again, from the same person, and in the same manner; expecting and disposing yourself to bear still harder things.

These contrary acts are needful to our perfection in all the virtues, because the exercises of which we have been speaking - manifold and efficacious as they are - will not suffice to eradicate the roots of sin.

Hence (to pursue the same example) although, when we receive an insult, we do not yield to the impulse of impatience, but, on the contrary, resist it by the three methods above described, yet, unless we accustom ourselves by many and repeated acts of the will to love contempt, and rejoice to be despised, we shall never overcome the sin of impatience, which springs from a regard for our own reputation and a shrinking from contempt.

And if the vicious root be left alive, it is ever springing up afresh; causing virtue to languish, and sometimes to perish utterly, and keeping us in continual danger of relapse upon the first opportunity which may present itself. Without these contrary acts, therefore, we shall never acquire a true habit of virtue.

And bear in mind also, that these acts should be so frequent and so numerous, as utterly to destroy the vicious habit, which, as it had obtained possession of our heart by repeated acts of sin, so by contrary acts must it be dislodged, to make way for the habit of virtue.

Again, a greater number of virtuous acts is requisite to form the habit of virtue than of evil ones to form the habit of vice; because the former are not, like the latter, assisted by our corrupt nature.

I would add to all that has been said, that if the virtue in which you are exercising yourself so require, you must also practice exterior acts conformable to the interior; as, for instance, words of love and meekness, and lowly services rendered to those who have in any way thwarted or slighted you.

And though all these acts, whether interior or exterior, should be, or should seem to you to be, feebly and faintly done, and, as it were, against your will, yet you must not on any account neglect them; for feeble as they may be, they will keep you safe and steadfast in the fight, and smooth before you the path to victory.

And stand always prepared and on your guard to resist the assaults of every passion, not only such as are violent and imperious, but the slightest and the gentlest; for these but open the way to the greater, by which habits of vice are gradually formed within us.

It has often happened, in consequence of the little care taken by some men to eradicate these lesser desires from their hearts, after they have overcome the more violent assaults of the same passion, that, when they have least expected it, their old enemies have fallen upon them again, and they have sustained a more complete and fatal defeat than had ever befallen them before.

Remember, again, to mortify and thwart your own wishes from time to time in lawful but not necessary things; for many benefits follow such discipline; it will prepare and dispose you more and more for self-mastery in other things; you will thus become expert and strong in the struggle with temptation; you will escape many a snare of the devil, and accomplish a work well pleasing to the Lord.

I speak plainly to you; if, in the way I have taught you, you will persevere faithfully in these holy exercises for self-reformation and self-mastery, I promise you that in a short time you will make great progress, and will become spiritual, not in name only, but in truth. But in no other manner do I bid you hope to attain to true holiness and spirituality, nor by any other exercises, however excellent in your estimation, though you should seem to be wholly absorbed in them, and to hold sweet colloquies with our Lord.

For, as I told you in the first chapter, true holiness and spirituality consists not in exercises which are pleasing to us and conformable to our nature, nor is it produced by these, but by such only as nail that nature, with all its works, to the cross, and, renewing the whole man by the practice of the evangelical virtues, unite him to his crucified Savior and Creator.

There can be no question that as habits of vice are formed by many and frequent acts of the superior will yielding itself to the sway of the sensual appetites, so, on the contrary, habits of evangelical virtue are acquired by the performance of frequent and repeated acts of conformity to the Divine Will, Which calls upon us to exercise ourselves now in one virtue, now in another.

For as our will, however fiercely assailed by sin or by the suggestions of our lower nature, can never become sinful or earthly unless it yield or incline itself to the temptation, so you will never attain to holiness and union with God, however powerfully called and mightily assailed by Divine grace and heavenly inspirations, unless by inward, and, if need be, by outward acts, your will be made conformable to His.

XIV: What must be done when the superior-will seems to be wholly stifled and overcome by the interim-will and by other enemies

If at times the superior will should seem to you powerless to resist the inferior and its other enemies because you do not feel within you an effectual will opposed to them, yet stand firm, and do not quit the field; for you must always account yourself victorious until you can clearly perceive that you have yielded.

For inasmuch as our superior will has no need of the inferior for the production of its acts, without its own consent it can never be compelled to yield, however sorely assaulted.

For God endued our will with such freedom and such strength, that were all the senses, all evil spirits, nay, the whole world itself, to arm and conspire to assault and oppress it with all their might, it could still, in spite of them, will or not will all that it wills or wills not; and that how often so-ever, when-so-ever, how-so-ever, and to what end so-ever it should please.

And if at any time your foes should so violently assail and press upon you as almost to stifle your will, so that it seems to have no breath to produce any opposing act of volition, yet do not lose courage, nor throw down your arms, but make use of your tongue in your defense, saying, "I yield not, I consent not;" like a man whose adversary is upon him and holds him down, and who, being unable to reach him with the point of his sword, strikes at him with the hilt; and as he tries to make a spring backwards to wound his enemy with the point, so do thou take refuge in the knowledge of yourself, the knowledge that you are nothing, and can do nothing, and with faith in God, Who can do all things, strike a blow at this hostile passion, saying: "Help me, Lord! help me, O my God! help me, Jesus, Mary! that I may not yield to this enemy."

You may also, when your enemy gives you time, call in your reason to assist the weakness of your will, by meditating upon various points, the consideration of which may give it strength and restore its breath to resist the enemy. For example: You are, perhaps, under some persecution or other trial, so sorely tempted to impatience, that your will, as it seems to you, cannot, or at least will not, endure it. Encourage it, then, by discussing with the reason such points as the following:

- ❖ Consider, first, whether you have given any occasion for the evil under which you are suffering and so have deserved it; for if you have done so, every rule of justice requires of you to bear patiently the wound which with your own hand you have inflicted on yourself.
- ❖ Second, if blameless in this particular instance think of your other sins, for which God has not yet chastised you, and for which you have not, as you should have done, duly punished yourself. Seeing, then, that God's mercy changes your deserved punishment, which should be eternal, into some light affliction which is but temporal, you should receive it, not willingly only, but thankfully.
- ❖ Third, should your offenses against the Divine Majesty seem to you to be light, and the penance you have endured for them heavy (a persuasion, however, which you should never allow yourself to entertain), you must remember that it is only through the straight gate of tribulation that you can enter into the kingdom of heaven.
- ❖ Fourth, that even were it possible to enter there by any other way, the law of love forbids you so much as to think of it, seeing that the Son of God, with all His friends and all His members, entered into that kingdom by a path strewed with thorns and crosses.
- ❖ Fifth, that which you have chiefly to consider, on this and all other occasions, is the will of God, Who, for the love He bears you, views with unspeakable complacency every act of virtue and mortification which, as His faithful and valiant soldier, you perform in requital of His love to you. And of this be assured, that the more unreasonable in itself the trial seems, and the more ignominious, by reason of the unworthiness of those from whom it comes, and so the more vexatious and the harder to be borne, so much the more pleasing will you be to the Lord, if in things so disordered in themselves, and therefore so bitter and repugnant to you, you can approve and love His Divine Will and Providence, in which all events, however adverse, are disposed after a most perfect rule and order.

XV: Some advice touching the manner of this warfare, and especially against whom, and with what resolution, it must be carried on

You see now after what manner you must fight in order to conquer self, and to adorn your soul with all virtues.

Know, furthermore, that to obtain a speedier and easier victory over your enemies, it is expedient, nay necessary, that you should fight against them daily, and especially against self-love, and learn to esteem as dear friends and benefactors all the insults and vexatious which the world can heap upon you. And it is because men know not the necessity of this daily warfare, and make too little account of it, that, as I said before, their victories are rare, difficult, imperfect, and unstable.

Moreover, I warn you that you must bring great steadfastness of soul to this conflict. And this gift you will readily obtain if you beseech it of God; considering, on the one hand, the undying hatred and fury of your enemies, and the vast multitude of their ranks and squadrons; and, on the other, how infinitely greater is the goodness of God and the love wherewith He loves you, and how much mightier, too, are the angels of heaven, and the prayers of the saints, which fight for us.

By this consideration have so many feeble women been en- abled to overcome and conquer all the power and wisdom of the world, all the assaults of the flesh, and all the fury of hell.

Therefore you must never be dismayed, though at times your enemy seem to be strengthening his array against you, though the struggle threaten to last your whole lifetime and though al- most certain falls menace you on every side; for know assuredly, that the whole strength and wisdom of our enemies is in the hands of our Divine Captain, in whose honor the battle is arrayed; Who, prizing us beyond measure, sure, and having Himself imperatively called us to the conflict, will never suffer you to be overcome. Nay more, He will Himself fight on your right hand, and will not fail in His own good time to subdue your foes before you; and this to your greater reward, if He should delay to give you the victory till the last day of your life.

This alone is your concern, to fight manfully, and never, however numerous your wounds, to lay down your arms or take to flight.

Lastly, that you fail not to fight courageously bear in mind that this is a conflict whence there is no escape; and that he who will not fight must needs be captured or slain. Moreover, we have to deal with enemies so powerful, and go filled with deadly hate, as to leave us no hope of either peace or truce.

XVI: In what manner the soldier-of-Christ should take the field early in the morning

"Not by might nor by power, but by my Spirit," says the Lord Almighty (Zechariah 4:6). On awaking in the morning, the first thing to be observed by your inward sight is the listed field in which you are enclosed, the law of the combat being that he who fights not must there lie dead forever. Here picture to yourself, on one side, your enemy (that evil inclination which you are already pledged to conquer) now standing before you, ready armed to wound and slay you; see also, on the right hand, your victorious Captain Jesus Christ, with His most holy Mother the Virgin Mary, and her beloved spouse Saint Joseph, and innumerable hosts of angels, especially Saint Michael the archangel; and, on the left hand, the infernal demon, with all his armies, ready to excite this passion and to persuade you to yield to it. Then shall you seem to hear a voice as of your guardian angel addressing you:

"You are to fight this day against this and other enemies of yours. Let not your heart fail, nor your spirit faint. Yield not on any account, neither for fear nor any other cause; for our Lord, your Leader, stands beside you with all His glorious hosts, and will do battle for you against all your enemies and will not suffer their form to prevail against you or to overcome you."

"Only stand firm; do violence to yourself, and endure the pain such violence will cause you. Cry unceasingly from the depths of your heart, and call upon the Lord, and so assuredly shalt you gain the victory. If you are weak and inexperienced, if your enemies are strong and manifold, manifold more are the succors of Him Who created and redeemed you, and mightier beyond all measure and comparison is your God, and more willing to save you than are all your enemies to destroy you."

"Fight valiantly then, and be not loathe to suffer; for it is this toilsome resistance to your evil inclinations, this painful struggle against evil habits, which shall gain you the victory, and win for you a treasure wherewith to purchase the kingdom of heaven, and unite your soul to God forever."

Begin the combat in the name of the Lord, with the weapons of self-distrust and trust in God, of prayer and spiritual exercises; and challenge to the battle your foe, that is, that inclination, whatever it be, which, according to the order above laid down, you have resolved to conquer. Do this, now by open resistance, now by deep abhorrence, or, again, by acts of the contrary virtue, wounding him again and again, even unto death, to give plea- sure to your Lord, Who is looking on, with the whole Church triumphant, to behold your conflict. I tell you again, you must not weary of the struggle, but re- member the obligation which lies on us all to serve and please God, and the absolute necessity of fighting in this battle, from which none can escape without wounds or death. I tell you, moreover, that if as a rebel you would fly from God, and give yourself over to the world and the delights of the flesh, you will still be forced, in spite of yourself, to labor in the sweat of your brow against many and many an adversary, who will pierce your heart with deadly anguish.

Consider, then, what folly it would be to incur all this toil and trouble, which does but lead to greater toil, and endless trouble and spiritual death, in order to avoid that which will soon be over, and which will lead us to eternal and infinite blessedness in the everlasting enjoyment of our God.

The Enemy's Deceptions

XXVII: Of the means employed by the Devil to assail and deceive those who desire to give themselves up to the practice of virtue, and those who are already entangled in the bondage of sin

You must know, that the devil is intent upon nothing but our ruin, and that he does not use the same method of assault with all persons. In order, then, to make known to you some of his modes of attack, his stratagems and devices, I will set before you several different conditions of men.

- ❖ Some remain in the service of sin without a thought of escape.
- ❖ Some would fain be free, but never make the attempt.
- ❖ Others think they are walking in the way of holiness, while they are wandering far from it.
- ❖ And lastly, some, after having attained unto holiness, fall into deeper perdition.

We will discourse separately of each.

XXVIII: Of the Devil's assaults and devices against those whom he holds in the bondage of sin

When the devil holds a man in the bondage of sin, his chief care is to blind his eyes more and more, and to avert from him everything which might lead to a knowledge of his most wretched condition.

And not only does he, by instilling contrary thoughts, drive from him all reflections and inspirations which call him to con- version, but, by affording him ready opportunities, he makes him fall into other and greater sins. Hence, the thicker and darker waxes his blindness, the more desperate and habitual becomes his course of sin; and thus, from blindness to deeper blindness, from sin to fouler sin, his wretched life will whirl on even unto death, unless God, by His grace, should intervene to save him. The remedy for one in this unhappy condition is, to be ready to give diligent heed to the thoughts and inspirations which call him from darkness to light, crying with all his heart to his Creator, "O Lord, help me; help me speedily; leave me not any longer in the darkness of sin." And let him not fail to repeat this cry for mercy over and over again in these or the like words.

If possible, let him have immediate recourse to some spiritual guide, and ask aid and counsel, that so he may be delivered from the power of the enemy.

And if he cannot do this at the moment, let him fly with all speed to the crucifix, prostrating himself before it; and asking mercy and aid also from the Mother of God.

On this speed does the victory depend, as you will learn in the next chapter.

XXIX: Of the arts and stratagems by which he holds in bondage those who knowing their misery, would fain be free; and how it is that our resolutions prove so often ineffectual

When a man begins to perceive the evil of his life, and to desire to change it, the devil often deludes and overcomes him by such means as these:

"Presently, presently."

"Cras, cras" (tomorrow, tomorrow) as the raven cries.

"I wish first to consider and dispatch this business, this perplexity, that I may then be able to give myself with greater tranquility to spiritual things."

This is a snare in which many men have been, and are still daily, entangled; and the cause of this is our own negligence and heedlessness, seeing that, in a matter touching the honor of God and the salvation of the soul, we neglect to seize instantly that effectual weapon: "Now, now;" wherefore "presently?"

"Today, today;" wherefore "tomorrow?" saying each one to himself:

"Even supposing this 'presently' and this 'tomorrow' should be granted to me, is it the way of safety and of victory to seek first to be wounded and to commit fresh disorders?"

You see, then, that the way to escape this snare, and that mentioned in the preceding chapter, and to subdue the enemy, is, to yield prompt obedience to all heavenly thoughts and inspirations.

Prompt obedience, I say, and not mere resolutions; for these are often fallacious, and many have been deceived thereby from various causes.

First. Because our resolutions are not founded upon self- distrust and trust in God. But our excessive pride, whence proceeds this blindness and delusion, prevents our perceiving it.

The light to see and the medicine to cure it both proceed from the goodness of God Who suffers us to fall that He may recall us thereby from self-confidence to confidence in Him alone, and from pride to self-knowledge.

Your resolutions, therefore, to be effectual, must be steadfast; and to be steadfast, they must be free from all self-confidence, and humbly based on confidence in God.

Second. When we are making our resolutions, we dwell on the beauty and excellence of virtue, which attracts our will, slack and feeble as it is; but when confronted by the difficulties which attend the attainment of virtue, the weak and untried will fail and draw back.

Learn, therefore, to love the difficulties which attend the attainment of all virtues more than even the virtues themselves, and use these difficulties in various measures to strengthen your will, if you desire in good earnest to acquire these virtues.

And know, that the more courageously and lovingly you shall embrace these difficulties, the more speedy and complete shall be your victory over self and all your other enemies.

Third. In our resolutions we too often look rather to our own advantage than to the will of God and the acquisition of the virtues He requires of us. This is frequently the case with resolutions made in times of great spiritual joy or acute sorrow, when we seem unable to find any relief but in a resolution to give ourselves wholly to God and to the practice of virtue.

To avoid this snare, take care in times of spiritual consolation to be very cautious and humble in your resolutions, especially in your vows and promises; and in tribulation let your resolution be to bear your cross patiently, according to the will of God, nay, to exalt it, refusing all earthly, and if so be even all heavenly consolation. Let your one desire, your one prayer, be that God would help you to bear all adverse things, keeping the virtue of patience unstained, and giving no displeasure to your Lord.

XXX: Of a delusion of those who imagine they are going onward to perfection

Our malignant foe, thus repulsed in his first and second assault and stratagem, has recourse to a third, which is, to turn away our attention from the enemies who are close at hand to injure and assail us, and to fill us with resolutions and desires after higher degrees of perfection.

Hence, we are continually being wounded; yet we pay no attention to our wounds, and looking upon these resolutions as already fulfilled, we take pride in them in various ways.

And while we cannot endure the least thing or the slightest word which crosses our will, we were our time in long meditations and resolutions to endure the acutest sufferings on earth or in purgatory for the love of God.

And because our inferior part feels no repugnance at these things in the distance, we flatter ourselves, miserable creatures as we are, into the conceit that we belong to the class of patient and heroic sufferers.

To avoid this snare, resolve to fight manfully against the enemies who are close at hand, and actually waging war against you. You will thus discover whether your resolutions are real or imaginary, weak or strong; and so you will go on to virtue and perfection by the beaten and royal road.

But against enemies who are not wont to trouble you I do not advise you to take up arms, unless there appear a probability of their making an attack at some future time. In this case it is lawful to make resolutions beforehand, that you may be found strong and prepared.

Do not, however, judge of your resolutions by their effects, even though you should have long and faithfully exercised your- self in virtue; but be very humble with regard to them; fear yourself and your own weakness, and trust in God, and seek His help by frequent prayer to strengthen and preserve you in all dangers, and especially from the very slightest presumption or self-confidence.

For in this case, though we may not be able to overcome some slight defects which our Lord sometimes leaves in us in order to greater, humility and self-knowledge, and for the protection of some virtue, we may yet be permitted to form purposes of aspiring to higher degrees of perfection.

XXXI: Of the Devil's assaults and stratagems in order to draw us away from the path of holiness

The fourth device of the Evil One, when he sees us advancing steadily towards holiness, is, to excite within us a variety of good desires, that by this means he may lead us away from the exercise of virtue into sin.

A sick person is perhaps bearing his illness with a patient will. The cunning adversary knows that by this means he may attain to a habit of patience; and he immediately sets before him all the good works which in a different condition he might be able to perform, and tries to persuade him that if he were but well he would be able to serve God better, and be more useful to himself and others.

Having once aroused such wishes within him, he goes on increasing them by degrees, till he makes him restless at the impossibility of carrying them into effect; and the deeper and stronger such wishes become, the more does this restlessness increase. Then the enemy leads him on gently, and with a stealthy step, to impatience at the sickness, not as sickness, but as a hindrance to those good works which he so anxiously desires to perform for some greater good.

When he has brought him thus far, with the same art he removes from his mind the end he had in view, to serve God and perform good works, and leaves him only the bare desire to be rid of his sickness. And then, if this does not happen according to his wish, he is so much troubled as to become actually impatient; and so unconsciously he falls from the virtue in which he was exercising himself into the opposite vice.

The way to guard against and resist this snare is, to be very careful, when in a state of trial, not to give way to desires after any good work, which, being out of your power to execute, would very probably disquiet you.

In such cases, resign yourself with all patience, resignation, and humility to the conviction that your desires would not have the effect you think, inasmuch as you are far more insignificant and unstable than you account yourself to be.

Or else believe that God, in His surer counsels, or on account of your unworthiness, is not pleased to accept this work at your hand, but will rather that you should patiently abase and humble yourself under the gentle and mighty hand of His will.

In like manner, if prevented by your spiritual father, or in any other way, from attending as frequently as you desire to your devotions, and especially Holy Communion, suffer not yourself to be troubled or disquieted by longings after them, but, casting off all that is your own, clothe yourself with the good pleasure of your Lord, saying within yourself:

"If the eye of Divine Providence had not perceived sin and ingratitude in me, I should not now be deprived of the blessing of receiving the most holy Sacrament; but since my Lord thus makes known to me my unworthiness, be His holy name for ever blessed and praised. I trust, O Lord, that in Your infinite loving-kindness You will so rule my heart, that it may please You in all things in doing or suffering Your will; that it may open before You, so that, entering into it spiritually, You may comfort and strengthen it against the enemies who seek to draw it away from You. Thus, may all be done as seems good in Your sight. My Creator and Redeemer, may Your will be now and ever my food and sustenance! This one favor only do I beg of You, O my Beloved, that my soul, freed and purified from everything displeasing to You, and adorned with all virtues, may be ever prepared for Your coming, and for whatsoever it may please You to do with me."

If you will observe these rules, know for certain that, when baffled in any good work which you have a desire to perform, be the hindrance from the devil, to disquiet you and turn you aside from the way of virtue, or be it from God, to make trial of your submission to His will, you will still have an opportunity of pleasing your Lord in the way most acceptable to Him. And herein consists true devotion, and the service which God requires of us.

I warn you, also, lest you grow impatient under trials, from whatever source proceeding, that in using the lawful means which God's servants are wont to use, you use them not with the desire and hope to obtain relief, but because it is the will of God that they should be used; for we know not whether His Divine Majesty will be pleased by their means to deliver us.

Otherwise you will fall into further evils; for if the event should not fulfill your purpose and desires, you will easily fall into impatience, or your patience will be defective, not wholly acceptable to God, and of little value.

Lastly, I would here warn you of a hidden deceit of our self- love, which is wont on certain occasions to cover and justify our faults. For instance, a sick man who has but little patience under his sickness conceals his impatience under the cover of zeal for some apparent good; saying, that his vexation arises not really from impatience under his sufferings, but is a reasonable sorrow, because he has incurred it by his own fault, or else because others are harassed or wearied by the trouble he gives them, or by some other cause.

In like manner, the ambitious man, who frets after some unattained honor, does not attribute his discontent to his own pride and vanity, but to some other cause, which he knows full well would give him no concern did it not touch himself. So neither would the sick man care if they, whose fatigue and trouble on his account seems to give him so much vexation, should have the same care and trouble on account of the sickness of another. A plain proof that the root of such men's sorrow is not concern for others, or anything else, but an abhorrence of everything that crosses their own will.

Therefore, to avoid this and other errors, bear patiently, as I have told you, every trial and every sorrow, from whatever cause arising.

XXXII: Of the above-named last assault and stratagem by which the Devil seeks to make the virtues we have acquired the occasions of our ruin

The cunning and malicious serpent fails not to tempt us by his artifices even by means of the very virtues we have acquired, that, leading us to regard them and ourselves with complacency, they may become our ruin; exalting us on high, that we may fall into the sin of pride and vainglory.

To preserve yourself from this danger, choose for your battlefield the safe and level ground of a true and deep conviction of your own nothingness, that you are nothing, that you know nothing, that you can do nothing, and have nothing but misery and sin, and deserve nothing but eternal damnation.

Entrench yourself firmly within the limits of this truth, and suffer not yourself to be enticed so much as a hair's breadth therefrom by any evil thought, or anything else that may befall you; knowing well that there are so many enemies, who would slay or wound you should you fall into their hands.

In order to acquit yourself well in this exercise of the true knowledge of your own nothingness, observe the following rule:

As often as you reflect upon yourself and your own works, consider always what you are of yourself, and not what you are by the aid of God's grace, and so esteem yourself as you shall thus find yourself to be.

Consider first the time before you were in existence, and you will see yourself to have been during all that abyss of eternity a mere nothing, and that you did nothing, and could have done nothing, towards giving yourself an existence.

Next consider the time since you did receive a being from the sole bounty of God. And here, also, if you leave to Him that which is His own (His continual care of you, which sustains you every moment of your life), what are you of yourself but still a mere nothing?

For, undoubtedly, were He to leave you for one moment to yourself, you would instantly return to that first nothingness from whence you were drawn by His Almighty Hand.

It is plain that, in the order of nature, and viewed in yourself alone, you have no reason to esteem yourself, or to desire the esteem of others.

Again, in the life of grace and the performance of good works, what good or meritorious deed could your nature perform by itself if deprived of Divine assistance? For, considering, on the other hand, the multitude of your past transgressions, and more- over the multitude of other sins from which God's compassionate Hand has alone withheld you, you will find that your iniquities, being multiplied not only by days and years, but by acts and habits of sin (one evil habit drawing another after it), would have swelled to an almost infinite amount, and so have made of you another infernal Lucifer. Hence, if you would not rob God of the praise of His goodness, but cleave faithfully to Him, you must learn day-by-day to think more humbly of yourself.

And be very careful to deal justly in this judgment of yourself, or it may do you no little injury.

For if in the knowledge of your own iniquity you surpass a man who, in his blindness, accounts himself to be something, you will lose exceedingly, and fall far below him in the action of the will, if you desire to be esteemed and regarded by men for that which you know yourself not to be.

If, then, you desire that the consciousness of your vileness and sinfulness should protect you from your enemies, and make you dear to God, you must not only despise yourself, as unworthy of any good and deserving of every evil, but you must love to be despised by others, detesting honors, rejoicing in shame, and stooping on all occasions to offices which others hold in contempt. You must make no account at all of their judgment, lest you be thereby deterred from this holy exercise. But take care that the end in view be solely your own humiliation and self-discipline, lest you be in any degree influenced by a certain lurking pride and spirit of presumption, which, under some specious pretext or other, often causes us to make little or no account of the opinions of others.

And should you perchance come to be loved, esteemed, or praised by others for any good gift bestowed on you by God, be not moved a single step thereby; but collect yourself steadily within the stronghold of this true and just judgment of yourself, first turning to God and saying to Him with all your heart:

"O Lord, never let me rob You of Your honor and the glory of Your grace; to You be praise and honor and glory, to me confusion of face."

And then say mentally of him who praises you: "Whence is it that he accounts me good, since truly my God and His works are alone good?"

For by thus giving back to the Lord that which is His own, you will keep your enemies afar off, and prepare yourself to receive greater gifts and favors from your God.

And if the remembrance of good works expose you to any risk of vanity, view them instantly, not as your own, but as God's; and say to them: "I know not how you did appear and originate in my mind, for you derived not your being from me; but the good God and His grace created, nourished, and preserved you. Him alone, then, will I acknowledge as your true and first Parent, Him will I thank, and to Him will I return all the praise."

Consider next, that not only do all the works which you have done fall short of the light which has been given you to know them, and the grace to execute them, but also that in them- selves they are very imperfect, and fall very short of that pure intention and due diligence and fervor with which they should be performed, and which should always accompany them.

If, then, you will well consider this, you will see reason rather for shame than for vain complacency, because it is but too true that the graces which we receive pure and perfect from God are sullied in their use by our imperfections. Again, compare your works with those of the saints and other servants of God; for by such comparison you will find that your best and greatest are of base alloy, and of little worth.

Next, measure them by those which Christ wrought for you in the mystery of His life, and of His continual Cross; and setting aside the consideration of His Divinity, view His works in them- selves alone; consider both the fervor and the purity of the love with which they were wrought, and you will see that all your works are indeed as nothing.

And lastly, if you will raise your thoughts to the Divinity and the boundless Majesty of your God, and the service which He deserves at your hands, you will see plainly that your works should excite in you not vanity but fear.

Therefore, in all your ways, in all your works, however holy they may be, you must cry unto your Lord with all your heart, saying: "God be merciful to me a sinner."

Further, I would advise you to be very reserved in making known the gifts which God may have bestowed on you; for this is almost always displeasing to your Lord, as He Himself plainly shows us in the following lesson.

Appearing once in the form of a child to a devout servant of His, she asked Him, with great simplicity, to recite the angelical salutation. He readily began: "*Ave Maria, gratia plena, Dominus tecum, benedicta tu in mulieribus,*" and then stopped, being unwilling to praise Himself in the words which follow. And while she was praying Him to proceed, He withdrew Himself from her, leaving His servant full of consolation because of the heavenly doctrine which, by His example, He had thus revealed to her.

Do you also learn to humble yourself, and to acknowledge yourself, with all your works, to be the nothing which you are.

This is the foundation of all other virtues. God, before we existed, created us out of nothing; and now that we exist through Him, He wills that the whole spiritual edifice should be built on this foundation the knowledge that of ourselves we are nothing. And the deeper we dig into this knowledge, the higher will the building rise. And in proportion as we clear away the earth of our own misery, the Divine Architect will bring solid stones for its completion.

And never imagine that you can dig deep enough; on the contrary, think this of yourself, that if anything belonging to a creature could be infinite, it would be your unworthiness.

With this knowledge, duly carried into practice, we possess all good; without it we are little better than nothing, though we should do the works of all the saints, and be continually absorbed in God.

O blessed knowledge, which makes us happy on earth, and blessed in heaven! O light, which, issuing from darkness, makes the soul bright and clear! O unknown joy, which sparkles amid our impurities! O nothingness, which, once known, makes us lords of all!

I should never weary of telling you this: if you would give praise to God, accuse yourself, and desire to be accused by others. Humble yourself with all, and below all, if you would exalt Him in yourself and yourself in Him.

Would you find Him? Exalt not yourself, or He will fly from you. Abase yourself to the utmost, and He will seek you and embrace you.

And the more you humble yourself in your own sight, and the more you delight to be accounted vile by others, and to be spurned as a thing abominable, the more lovingly will He esteem and embrace you. Account yourself unworthy of so great a grace bestowed on you by your God, Who suffered shame for you in order to unite you to Himself. Fail not to return Him continual thanks; and be grateful to those who have been the occasion of your humiliation, and still more to those who have trampled you under their feet, thinking that you have endured it reluctantly, and not with your own goodwill. Yet were it even so, you must suffer no outward token of reluctance to escape you.

If, notwithstanding all these considerations, which are only too true, the cunning of the devil and our own ignorance and evil inclinations should yet prevail over us, so that thoughts of self-exaltation will still molest us and make an impression on our hearts, then is the time to humble ourselves the more profoundly in our own sight; for we see by this proof that we have advanced but a little way in the spiritual life and in true self-knowledge, inasmuch as we are unable to free ourselves from those annoyances which spring from the root of our empty pride. So shall we extract honey from the poison and healing from the wound.

About the Author

Scott Smith is a Catholic author, attorney, and theologian. He and his wife Ashton are the parents of four wild-eyed children and live in their hometown of New Roads, Louisiana. He is currently serving as the Chairman of the Men of the Immaculata, the Grand Knight of his local Knights of Columbus council, and a co-host of the Catholic Nerds Podcast. Smith has served as a minister and teacher far and wide: from Angola, Louisiana's maximum security prison, to the slums of Kibera, Kenya.

Smith is the author of the first pro-life horror novel, *The Seventh Word*. His other books include *Pray the Rosary with St. Pope John Paul II*, *The Catholic ManBook*, *Everything You Need to Know About Mary But Were Never Taught*, and *Blessed is He Who ...* (Biographies of Blesseds).

Check out more of his writing and courses below ...

More from Scott Smith

Scott regularly contributes to his blog, "The Scott Smith Blog" at www.thescottsmithblog.com, WINNER of the 2018-2019 Fisher's Net Award for Best Catholic Blog:

Scott's other books can be found at his publisher's, Holy Water Books, website, holywaterbooks.com, as well as on Amazon.

His other books on theology and the Catholic faith include *The Catholic ManBook*, *Everything You Need to Know About Mary But Were Never Taught*, and *Blessed is He Who …* (Biographies of Blesseds). More on these below …

His fiction includes *The Seventh Word*, a pro-life horror novel, and the *Cajun Zombie Chronicles*, the Catholic version of the zombie apocalypse.

Scott also recently authored a series of prayer journals with his wife. *The Pray, Hope, & Don't Worry* Prayer Journal to Overcome Stress and Anxiety:

Scott L. Smith, Jr.

Scott has also produced courses on the Blessed Mother and Scripture for All Saints University.

Learn about the Blessed Mary from anywhere and learn to defend your mother! It includes over six hours of video plus a free copy of the next book ... Enroll Now!

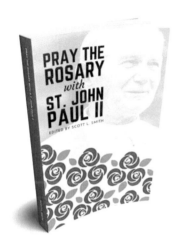

Pray the Rosary with St. John Paul II

St. John Paul II said "the Rosary is my favorite prayer." So what could possibly make praying the Rosary even better? Praying the Rosary with St. John Paul II!

This book includes a reflection from John Paul II for every mystery of the Rosary. You will find John Paul II's biblical reflections on the twenty mysteries of the Rosary that provide practical insights to help you not only understand the twenty mysteries but also live them.

St. John Paul II said "The Rosary is my favorite prayer. A marvelous prayer! Marvelous in its simplicity and its depth. In the prayer we repeat many times the words that the Virgin Mary heard from the Archangel, and from her kinswoman Elizabeth."

St. John Paul II said "the Rosary is the storehouse of countless blessings." In this new book, he will help you dig even deeper into the treasures contained within the Rosary.

You will also learn St. John Paul II's spirituality of the Rosary: "To pray the Rosary is to hand over our burdens to the merciful hearts of Christ and His mother."

"The Rosary, though clearly Marian in character, is at heart a Christ-centered prayer. It has all the depth of the gospel message in its entirety. It is an echo of the prayer of Mary, her perennial Magnificat for the work of the redemptive Incarnation which began in her virginal womb."

Take the Rosary to a whole new level with St. John Paul the Great! St. John Paul II, *pray for us!*

Scott L. Smith, Jr.

What You Need to Know About Mary But Were Never Taught

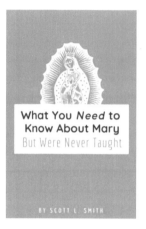

Give a robust defense of the Blessed Mother using Scripture. Now, more than ever, every Catholic needs to learn how to defend their mother, the Blessed Mother. Because now, more than ever, the family is under attack and needs its Mother.

Discover the love story, hidden within the whole of Scripture, of the Father for his daughter, the Holy Spirit for his spouse, and the Son for his MOTHER.

This collection of essays and the All Saints University course made to accompany it will demonstrate through Scripture how the Immaculate Conception of Mary was prophesied in Genesis.

It will also show how the Virgin Mary is the New Eve, the New Ark, and the New Queen of Israel.

Catholic Nerds Podcast

As you might have noticed, Scott is obviously well-credentialed as a nerd. Check out Scott's podcast: the Catholic Nerds Podcast on iTunes, Podbean, Google Play, and wherever good podcasts are found!

The Catholic ManBook

Do you want to reach Catholic Man LEVEL: EXPERT? *The Catholic ManBook* is your handbook to achieving Sainthood, manly Sainthood. Find the following resources inside, plus many others:

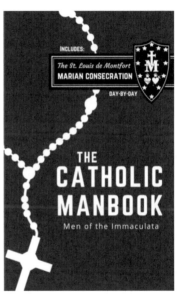

- Top Catholic Apps, Websites, and Blogs
- Everything you need to pray the Rosary
- The Most Effective Daily Prayers & Novenas, including the Emergency Novena
- Going to Confession and Eucharistic Adoration like a boss!
- Mastering the Catholic Liturgical Calendar

The Catholic ManBook contains the collective wisdom of The Men of the Immaculata, of saints, priests and laymen, fathers and sons, single and married. Holiness is at your fingertips. Get your copy today.

This edition also includes a revised and updated St. Louis de Montfort Marian consecration. Follow the prayers in a day-by-day format.

The Seventh Word
The FIRST Pro-Life Horror Novel!

Pro-Life hero, Abby Johnson, called it "legit scary ... I don't like reading this as night! ... It was good, it was so good ... it was terrifying, but good."

The First Word came with Cain, who killed the first child of man. The Third Word was Pharaoh's instruction to the midwives. The Fifth Word was carried from Herod to Bethlehem. One of the Lost Words dwelt among the Aztecs and hungered after their children.

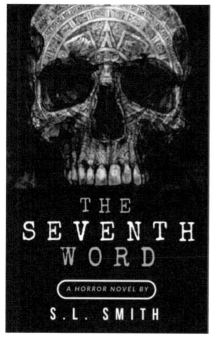

Evil hides behind starched white masks. The ancient Aztec demon now conducts his affairs in the sterile environment of corporate medical facilities. An insatiable hunger draws the demon to a sleepy Louisiana hamlet.

There, it contracts the services of a young attorney, Jim David, whose unborn child is the ultimate object of the demon's designs. Monsignor, a mysterious priest of unknown age and origin, labors unseen to save the soul of a small town hidden deep within Louisiana's plantation country, nearly forgotten in a bend of the Mississippi River.

You'll be gripped from start to heart-stopping finish in this page-turning thriller.

With roots in Bram Stoker's Dracula, this horror novel reads like Stephen King's classic stories of towns being slowly devoured by an unseen evil and the people who unite against it.

The book is set in southern Louisiana, an area the author brings to life with compelling detail based on his local knowledge.

Blessed is He Who ...
Models of Catholic Manhood

You are the average of the five people you spend the most time with, so spend more time with the Saints! Here are several men that you need to get to know whatever your age or station in life. These short biographies will give you an insight into how to live better, however you're living.

From Kings to computer nerds, old married couples to single teenagers, these men gave us extraordinary examples of holiness:

- Pier Giorgio Frassati & Carlo Acutis – Here are two ex-traordinary **young men**, an athlete and a computer nerd, living on either side of the 20th Century
- Two men of royal stock, Francesco II and Archduke Eu-gen, lived lives of holiness despite all the world conspir-ing against them.
- There's also the **simple husband and father**, Blessed Luigi. Though he wasn't a king, he can help all of us treat the women in our lives as queens.

Blessed Is He Who ... Models of Catholic Manhood explores the lives of six men who found their greatness in Christ and His Bride, the Church. In six succinct chapters, the authors, noted historian Brian J. Costello and theologian and at-torney Scott L. Smith, share with you the uncommon lives of exceptional men who will one day be numbered among the Saints of Heaven, men who can bring all of us closer to sainthood.

Made in the USA
Thornton, CO
04/14/23 17:51:08